I0114919

Rethinking Contemporary Indian Polity

Rethinking Contemporary Indian Polity

Editor

Shalini Saxena

Vij Books India Pvt Ltd
New Delhi (India)

Published by

Vij Books India Pvt Ltd
(Publishers, Distributors & Importers)
2/19, Ansari Road
Delhi – 110 002
Phones: 91-11-43596460, 91-11-47340674
e-mail: vijbooks@rediffmail.com
web : www.vijbooks.com

First Published in India in 2018

Copyright © 2018, Editor

ISBN: 978-93-88161-10-7 (Hardback)

ISBN: 978-93-88161-11-4 (ebook)

All rights reserved.

No part of this book may be reproduced, stored in a retrieval system, transmitted or utilized in any form or by any means, electronic, mechanical, photocopying, recording or otherwise, without the prior permission of the copyright owner. Application for such permission should be addressed to the publisher.

The views expressed in this book are of the author in his personal capacity and do not represent the views of the institution he belong to.

To my Mother Smt Indra Saxena
I miss you in every moment of my life....

Contents

Preface

This book is designed to serve on the issues of contemporary political scenario for political scientists, political science students, research scholars, media persons and for the people who have interest in contemporary politics. This reference book talks about the recent developments of contemporary politics predominantly after 2014. This volume is divided into nine chapters and each chapter contemplates comprehensively on different aspects of existing political situation.

The introductory chapter on Rethinking Contemporary Indian Polity is contributed by the editor herself, which conveys an overall glimpse of present political situation specifically after 2014 when the new government under the able leadership of Prime Minister Shri Narendra Modi took charge.

Second chapter, which is contributed by Dr Jyotika Teckchandani, is Contemporary Government: Diaspora Policy. It is based on the present government diaspora policy. This chapter explores the changing meaning of diaspora and reflects upon the nature and features of Diaspora Policy of Prime Minister Modi and its impact on the changing perception about India in the world.

Chapter three Securing the Environment and promoting Gender Security is written by Mr V C Shushant Parashar. It gives gender based perspective on how security of the environment promotes gender security. This chapter also considers whether adequate options exist for women to participate to improve human security via environment security in the changing face of climate change in the recent times.

Chapter four Social Welfare Measures in Contemporary Indian Polity is contributed by Dr Nandini Sahay. This chapter presents a complete picture on the current government's social welfare schemes and programmes which cater to the needs of the weaker sections of the society including women, children, handicapped, aged, Scheduled Castes and Scheduled Tribes etc.

Chapter five is written by Dr Suresh Chandra Patel on Rethinking Indian Federalism: Issues and Challenges. It explains about the need of rethinking on the Indian federalism as the success of Indian democracy depends on the federal structure of India.

Sixth chapter is Situating India on the World Map: India's Rise Narrative and Rethinking Cohen's World Geopolitical Order, which is written by Ms Deblina Mukherjee, focuses on the geopolitical visions and world views, geopolitical code constructions and policy formulations by the strategic elite which gave India the new image from the 1990s onwards and in contemporary times.

Chapter seven which is on Maoist Movement and its Effect on Indian Political System is contributed by Ms Puspitarani Bardhan. This chapter narrates about the problem of Maoism and failure of the policy and plan meant for the development of the people of the country as the present NDA government also believes that the Maoist and Maoist problem need to be solved in the interest of the development of the people of India.

Chapter eight is National Security: Role of Energy in terms of Oil and Natural Gas: Future Prospects with reference to India is written by Mr. Rajneesh Kumar. It gives an overview on a comprehensive discipline encompassing not only the hard power but also the soft power in the form of various other politico-diplomatic and technological factors related to India as an independent politico-economic power to realize its national interests by practicing strong diplomacy in the present times.

The last chapter is on Local Democracy: Issues and challenges of economic development in south Asia is contributed by Dr

Vadranam Suresh. It elucidates on Sustainable Development Goals (SDGs) with an increased focus on context specific and local economic development as a driver of poverty reduction, women's empowerment and 'inclusive growth with quality work' the world over. This chapter gives a preview of present government policy to ensure that local economic development feature prominently in the strategy for implementing the new SDGs which promise to 'leave no one behind' and ensuring effective and accountable government 'at all levels'. Shri Narendra Modi's slogan *Sabka Saath, Sabka Vikas* explains it all.

The book ends with the details of its contributors.

–Dr Shalini Saxena.

Acknowledgements

I would like to express my gratitude to the many people who saw me through this book; to all those who provided support, talked things over, read, wrote, offered comments, allowed me to quote their remarks and assisted in the editing, proofreading and designing of the book.

First of all, I would like to thank my father Shri Satish Chandra Saxena for his blessings. He always encouraged me to aim high. Above all I thank my husband Vivek, my kids Tathagat and Niranjani and my mother in law Dr Sudha Saxena, who supported and encouraged me despite all the time it took me away from them.

I would like to thank my brothers for facilitating me in the process of creating of this book.

Thanks to Mr Rohan Vij, my publisher who encouraged me.

My gratitude to Amity University, Noida, for providing me access to exposure and freedom to work.

Thanks to God, without his support this book would never find its way. Last but not the least, I seek forgiveness of all those who have been with me over the course of time and whose names I have failed to mention.

–Dr. Shalini Saxena

Rethinking Contemporary Indian Polity
An Introduction

Dr. Shalini Saxena

India was coxswained to a new government in 2014. This government has brought out many changes. On May 26, 2018 the government completed four years in power. Narendra Modi became the Prime Minister of India riding high on the aspirations and expectations of people, who waited for 'achhe din' - the slogan which propelled the Bharatiya Janata Party to become the first political party in 30 years to win a majority on its own in the Lok Sabha. Four years down the line, the current government faces serious challenges even as the BJP has been on an election winning spree.

The efficient use of technology in governance, programs to promote digital awareness among citizens, the launch of Jan Dhan Yojana are amongst the many initiatives taken by the government which have proved to be successful. The biggest change seen in the last few years is the presence of a corruption-free government. The government has established a good rapport with other countries, both near and far. FDI is growing at a healthy rate with the government establishing norms to reduce corruption and simultaneously assisting the young entrepreneurs to develop and thus develop the nation in turn. Our government has initiated the Swachh Bharat Abhiyaan drive which aims to make India clean. Skill India training and use of solar power are some of the good initiatives taken by our government so far.

As the Modi government enters the fifth year of its term, its monetary report card looks great. The administration has numerous accomplishments shockingly. In 2013, the economy was in an awful shape: development had drooped to beneath 6 percent, rupee collided with 68.85 to the dollar on August 28, 2013 after the QE decrease declaration, the twin shortage issue – high financial and current record shortfalls - rendered Indian economy very powerless and swelling was seething over 10 percent.

Outside institutional speculators (FIIs) place India in the 'delicate five' gathering BIITS (Brazil, India, Indonesia, Turkey and South Africa) and sold intensely, affecting the cash and securities exchanges.

Facilitate, approach loss of motion in the last period of the UPA government had affected business certainty and financial development.

As the Modi government enters the fourth year, the economy is in a vastly improved shape. In the developing markets, India is in a large scale sweet spot. Indian GDP development in 2017-18 evaluated to ascend to 7.4 percent is probably going to be the most noteworthy among huge economies on the planet.

The IMF a year ago alluded to India as the 'splendid spot in the melancholy worldwide economy'. Because of the financial solidification in progressive spending plans, the monetary shortfall has been conveyed down to 3.2 percent. Current record deficiency at 1 percent is not an issue by any means.

The rupee has fortified to around 68.71 to the dollar. Over the most recent 3 years, retail expansion found the middle value of 5.2 percent. By and by, the CPI expansion is underneath 3 percent. Sends out, following three years of dreary execution, have begun getting and India has risen as one of the biggest beneficiaries of FDI on the planet.

The share trading system is at record highs and speculators, both outside and residential, are emptying cash into the market. This move from "delicate five to fantastic few" is a great reputation.

The economy has immediately recuperated from demonetization and now remonetisation is contributing considerably to monetary development. On the foundation front, street and power segments can brag of amazing additions. GST will be a reality.

Note that private venture is yet to get and the keeping money framework is reeling under the overwhelming weight of focused on resources. Despite the fact that the legislature can guarantee that the high NPA is a heritage issue, actually it is chocking development in the economy.

The present worldwide condition is positive. Worldwide exchange is getting. In India, financing costs are drifting down and speculation can be relied upon to get soon.

Achievements have been many in this short span of three years and so have been the flaws. Three years into its five-year term and the Modi government's way to deal with social approach stays indistinct. This positively is, partially, an impression of the numerous and regularly conflicting pulls and weights of building a welfare state in India. Be that as it may, it is likewise an impression of the administration's absence of political creative ability and capacity to construct an agreement around basic issues like wellbeing and training.

In 2014, when the National Democratic Alliance (NDA) government rode to control, many had expected (with reckoning or fear contingent upon which side of the ideological fence you sit on) that the legislature would profoundly adjust the engineering for welfare. In fact, ahead of schedule into its term, the administration set about the undertaking of recognizing (and removing) itself from the United Progressive Alliance's (UPA) rights-based welfare approach by situating its way to deal with social strategy as "strengthening" contrary to the UPA's "privilege" approach. Supplanting the broken and wasteful welfare conveyance framework with the misleadingly exquisite money exchange model was a basic part of the strengthening story. To do this, the administration's initially errand was proportional up the immediate advantage exchange (DBT) pilots with the JAM (Jan

Dhan, Aadhaar, Mobile) trinity as its establishment.

Advance, be that as it may, has been moderate. The objective in 2014 was for DBT to cover 536 plans crosswise over 65 services and offices. By December 2016, just 84 conspires crosswise over 17 offices and services were utilizing DBT. Additionally, the pace of cash exchanges through DBT has backed off. By December 2016, just 45% of the 2016-17 Government of India (GOI) assignment for LPG appropriations and 62% for the National Social Assistance Program were exchanged through DBT. And keeping in mind that the administration is attempting to reveal the DBT, the PM has swung to the UPAs "qualification" projects to react to post-demonetisation stuns to the country economy. In his December 31 discourse, the PM conferred his administration to actualizing the maternity benefits program, a key arrangement of the National Food Security Act. Add to this, the MGNREGA, which was given another rent of life not long ago because of dry spell conditions in many parts of India, has as of late gotten a supplementary concede by virtue of the expanded request in December. By early January 2017, the center had discharged Rs. 55,076 crore for MGREGA – the most noteworthy distribution so far since the program was propelled.

The absence of political agreement likewise uncovered the constraints of the money contention. The push to money exchanges comes from the conviction that money exchanges are an answer for the states proceeded with inability to convey administrations. However, as the DBT experience is starting to uncover, money is not a substitute for a fizzled state framework. Getting the money engineering right requires arranging complex administration undertakings like getting focusing on right, adjusting to market variances, managing supply limitations and building a working keeping money framework. Instead of being a substitute, viable money exchanges require a refined and fit state hardware to bolster it. The inability to perceive this, particularly as requires a Universal Basic Income become louder, and put resources into building state limit is this present government's most noteworthy blunder. The UPA left the vast majority of its qualification plans, including the MGNREGA, in dire need of enhanced execution. As opposed to concentrate on getting execution right, the conflicting messages from the administration have additionally debilitated these projects.

Wage instalments under MGNREGA are a decent case of this. In 2016-17, when the legislature required MGNREGA to perform, 53% of instalments were postponed by between 15-90 days.

Wellbeing is the greater causality. The National Health Policy has vanished without a follow. In the 2016 spending plan, another medical coverage plan was declared. After a year, this is still to be executed. And keeping in mind that administration talk proposes a move in need toward protection, there is no level-headed discussion on the most proficient method to handle complex issues of direction and quality. Then again, the National Health Mission (NHM), the present lead program for fortifying essential wellbeing frameworks, which still records for half of the inside's wellbeing spending plan, is flopping. What's more, in spite of developing confirmation of a genuine emergency in the nature of essential care, from specialist non-appearance to low exertion, absence of utilization of treatment conventions, over-solution and abuse of patients, the legislature is demonstrating no direness to change the NHM. To be reasonable, the present emergency in human services is not the making of this administration. In any case, the absence of a reasonable vision and methodology on the most proficient method to handle this emergency, particularly with regards to the talk of strengthening, is a genuine disappointment.

Rudimentary instruction has had a moderately better run. The need to earnestly handle the low learning levels in India's grade schools is presently generally perceived and despite the fact that the National Education Policy has been conceded to yet another board, the sense of duty regarding enhance learning results has been plainly expressed. Right now, the exertion is centred on measuring learning. The Niti Aayog is propelling a school quality list while the training service is planning to attempt a learning statistics. Estimation is important yet its convenience relies on the framework's capacity to utilize estimation as an analytic instrument to change the instructing learning process. For the occasion, there is little clearness from the legislature on how it expects to utilize these evaluations.

The issue is muddled by the way that the present arranging and planning procedure is not intended to organize learning. Arranging keeps on being founded on school framework objectives and learning centred projects get almost no financing. In 2014-15 (most recent accessible figures) 78% of the Sarva Shiksha Abhiyan (the administration lead plot for rudimentary training) spending plan was assigned to foundation and educator pay rates. The two details that emphasis particularly on fuelling learning-centred development – (advancement and learning upgrade program) got under 1% of the SSA spending plan. What's more, this is the one zone that has seen the most cuts – in 2014-15 just 13% of assets asked for these exercises were endorsed. This expanded to 25% in 2015-16. Many state governments are presently starting to try different things with various methods for changing classroom practices to enhance learning. These should be upheld, contemplated and scaled. Be that as it may, the nonattendance of assets and the proceeded with concentrate on school framework in arrangements and spending plans is a genuine hindrance.

At last, no exchange on the Modi government's social arrangement approach is finished without say of two issues on which the PM has staked critical political capital – Swachh Bharat and co-agent federalism.

On Swachh Bharat, the abnormal state political duty has made sanitation best need the nation over. Be that as it may, the essential plan and approach of the Swachh Bharat Mission (SBM) is defective. As is generally recognized, add up to sanitation is just accomplished when groups perceive the requirement for sanitation and request sanitation administrations. Building mindfulness for sanitation and making a request through maintained group engagement is accordingly basic and neighbourhood governments are the suitable institutional instrument to accomplish this. Instead of reinforcing neighbourhood governments, the SBM is planned as a top down program executed by civil servants.

Thus, even as cash is being spent on can development – 98% of the 2016-17 Swachh Bharat Mission-Gramin (SBM-G) use has been on latrine development (IHHL) – the genuine test of conduct change remains. It ought to be noticed that there are separate figures for SBM-U (urban), which are surprisingly more terrible off as far as spending and execution.

One representation of this is the low levels of use on mindfulness raising. In 2016-17, till January tenth just Rs. 56 crore, which is 1% of the aggregate use on the plan, had been spent for mindfulness raising exercises. What's more, notwithstanding weight to meet targets toilets are being built for the most part by cajoling natives through requests debilitating to withhold proportion and power supplies, government has stood silent on inflation and rising prices of essential commodities. No stance has been taken upon economic defaulters and the government remains silent on controversial issues and should try to sort them out before things get out of hand. There is dissent among central universities which needs to be sorted out immediately. The government has fallen short on its promise of bringing black money.

The current government should take advantage of the opportunities that come with the tide. Reduction in global oil prices, recession in the global market, and a downward spiral in Chinese GDP growth rate, infrastructure development and backing Make in India etc. are some of the many opportunities the current government should cash in. The government should take care of the rising threats such as delay in implementation of business policies can undermine the economy of the country, a delay in acting against those who are corrupt will affect the image of the current government. With each passing second, time is becoming a scarce commodity to act upon the promises made during the elections. Environmental issues such as water shortages, climate change etc. have a major issue. The government has a lot in its hand and time running out. Performance needs to enhance by addressing the weak areas. Threats need to be converted into opportunities and the prevailing opportunities need to cash in. The government needs to ensure that policies get implemented fast and their impact is felt by the public. Extremist elements need to rein in so that more focus is given to development. The current year is of utmost significance in shaping our government's legacy to have another chance in 2019. It is inappropriate to utilize these triumphs to overlook the shortcomings in the economy, similarly as it is inappropriate to hail these shortcomings and say the victories don't make a difference. The absence of occupations, non-existent venture and weak monetary segment are not declarations to the disappointment of this legislature on the financial approach front. There's a considerable measure that the Modi government still needs to do to support this development.

All the chapters included in the book will explicitly explain about the contemporary Indian Polity.

Modi Government, Development and Diaspora

Dr. Jyotika Teckchandani

Abstract

'Diaspora' has emerged as a new concept in the arena of international politics. From its original negative victim hood sense to overlapping with the meaning of 'migrants', today diaspora has a positive connotation. A nation with strong diaspora community now looks forward to its diasporic community to contribute to national well-being. With globalization, shrinking of time and space and growing inter-connectedness of the world, the diaspora is playing an important role in integrating of the nation in the emerging globalized world order.

Mr. Narendra Modi is the first Indian Prime Minister who has brought the linkage between Indian diasporic community and development of the country. This paper, will explore the changing meaning of diaspora and would be reflecting upon the nature and features of Diaspora Policy of Prime Minister Modi and its impact on the changing perception about India in the world.

Keywords: Diaspora, India, PM Modi, Foreign Policy, Remittances, Investment

Introduction

The term Diaspora is derived from the Greek words "dia", which means "through," and "kpeiro," which means "to scatter". Literally, "Diaspora" means "scattering" or "dispersion."[1] The term originally referred to the dispersion of Jews after their exile from Babylon in the 6th Century BC, and later to describe all the Jewish people scattered in exile outside Palestine. Today, the word has evolved to classify any group of people who are dispersed or scattered away from their home country with a distinct collective memory and a myth of return.[2]

Indian diaspora refers to the people of Indian origin as well as Indian citizens living abroad for work or business. Indian Diaspora is used to describe the people who migrated from territories that are currently within the borders of India. In the last few decades' number of highly professional, semi-skilled and unskilled workers, students have shifted abroad. The Indian Diaspora numbers around 25 million people and is considered by the United Nations to be the world's largest such community spread across 136 countries[3] across the globe. Considering its size and expansion, it is aptly mentioned in the High-Level Committee Report on Indian Diaspora by the Government of India, "The Sun never sets in the Indian Diaspora".[4]

Due to globalization and liberalization of a global economic system coupled with the rapid advancement of transport and communication technologies that have reduced time and space that have in turn intensified their socio-economic, political and cultural ties very stronger with their origin countries. Hence, not only have Diasporas attained due importance at the international level, but also in the domestic political and economic affairs of home countries than ever before. Hence, Diasporas being transnational communities have become important non-state actors as well as deciding factors in international political and economic relations.[5]

They have emerged as an 'inexorable link' between their home and host lands. Diasporas are recognized as 'soft power' in the realm of foreign policy strategy and also as a catalyst for economic development of countries of origin besides their active role in the host countries.[6] For instance, in the economic sphere, the Chinese Diaspora has been seen as a propelling force for its emergence as an economic superpower. In the political sphere, the Jewish Diaspora has a strong grip over the US and European

Union in terms of shaping their strategic relationship with Israel.

Indian Government's Diaspora Policy from 1947 till 2014

Jawaharlal Nehru, India's first Prime Minister, pursued a policy of "active dissociation" from the Indian diaspora.[7] He was concerned that connecting with and advocating for, them would impair the sovereignty of host countries.[8] This was in sync with India's foreign policy which was guided by Nehruvian ideals of anti-imperialism and racial apartheid[9], respect for Sovereignty and non-alignment. Jawaharlal Nehru categorically announced that ethnic Indians who chose to remain abroad would consider themselves as citizens or nationals of their respective host lands.[10] In fact, they were encouraged to integrate with host culture and fight for the liberation of their adopted lands. His model of engagement with the Indian diaspora involved having them shun deep emotional ties and bond with India and to completely merge with the local culture.

Indians, especially those whose acquired citizenship of other country, were looked upon with disdain, as outcasts who deserted their own country — some even their families — to settle abroad in lieu of better opportunities over there. They were looked upon as a distant entity who were in no way related to Indian interests.

The Jawaharlal Nehru Government's approach to the diaspora community was a low-key affair. It was such that the NRIs received shame for having abandoned their motherland. Those days India was thriving to establish good connections globally as it needed support and aid for development. India's foreign policy was, thus, structured according to the model of non-intervention so much that the diaspora community could not even reach out to the Indian Government even in times of crisis or emergency.

Nehru's policy left a bitter taste for generations among Indian-origin communities abroad. His cold view of overseas Indians was encapsulated in a comment made in India's Parliament in 1957: "If they adopt the nationality of that country, we have no concern with them. Sentimental concern there is, but politically they cease to be Indian nationals."[11]

Lal Bahadur Shastri entered into an agreement with Srimavo Bandaranaike[12] to resolve the question of Tamils in Sri Lanka. Otherwise, the Nehruvian trend was continued and extended to till 1980 by successive governments. For years, we interacted with Indian community only on national days or other important occasions. Problems of the diaspora were never given importance. Later, in spite of a change of focus in the India's foreign policy from Nehruvian idealism to realism under the regime of Indira Gandhi, there was no change of position in the Diaspora policy or the Indian economic foreign policy. In fact, she made herself particularly unpopular during the East African Indian crisis of 1968-1972. However, owing to oil shocks and Balance of Payment crisis, the government pushed for a remittance –centric approach, especially for the Gulf Indian.[13]

Under the regime of Rajiv Gandhi, there was a boost in Diaspora policy. He offered support at Fiji Indian crisis in 1986. Besides, having realized Indian Diaspora as a strategic asset, he invited Indian diasporic talents like Sam Pitroda to participate in nation-building and took administrative measures like the establishment of Indian Overseas department in 1984.[14]

After the end of Cold War, the emergence of a multi-polar centric foreign policy, a structural shift in the global economy and the relentless foreign reserve crisis of Indian economy in the 1990s, facilitated the Indian government led by Narasimha Rao to announce drastic economic reforms such as Liberalization, Privatization, Globalization (LPG).[15] On the advent of the new economic model, the Indian Diaspora was able to participate in the plethora of economic opportunities of the unregulated and open Indian economy. It resolved the foreign currency crisis due to substantial investment and remittance from the Indian Diaspora. Subsequently, the Indian government changed its outlook towards Diaspora and reviewed its Diaspora policy. [16]

At the same time, there were no constructive steps or consistent and clear-cut policies to deal with or tap the overseas Indians until the coming of National Democratic Alliance government led by BJP. It was under NDA that Pravasi Bharatiya

Divas was first launched in 2003 (Since 2003, every year we celebrate Pravasi Bharatiya Divas on January 9th, a day on which Mahatma Gandhi returned to India from South Africa.) The NDA government of PM Atal Bihari Vajpayee decided to celebrate it annually by holding events including bestowing awards on the prominent members of Indian diaspora (Pravasi Bharatiya Samman Awards). Also, appointment of High-Level Committee on Indian Diaspora, launching of PIO card scheme, offering Dual citizenship (OCI) and so on. The subsequent UPA government established a separate Ministry of Overseas Indian Affairs which has taken several initiatives for engaging the Diaspora.

PM Modi and Diaspora

Mr. Modi is the first Indian Prime Minister who has brought the linkage between Indian diasporic community and development of the country. Diaspora has become an important feature of Modi's foreign policy. Modi appreciates the Indian diaspora's as he travels the world.

The Indian foreign policy is increasingly characterized by what has come to be known as "the Modi doctrine". The doctrine, while operating within the broad framework of Indian foreign policy, injects a new sense of vigour, commitment, pragmatism, flexibility and action-oriented policies to achieve its twin purpose of national security and economic development.

The unprecedented foreign trips undertaken by our Prime Minister during last three years has, an important dimension of galvanizing the role and significance of Indian diasporic community in the development of the country, in addition to attracting the global investment, aids and technology.

For Modi, the Diaspora is an 'asset' rather than a 'liability' and India's intellectual power beyond borders is 'brain gain' and not 'brain drain'.[17] He asserts that India has been a net giver of countless benefits to the world at large.

This is reflected in his special outreach to Indian communities during his visits to the United States, the United Kingdom,

Australia, Canada and Singapore, Israel, and even with respect to the Indian workers in the Middle Eastern countries like the United Arab Emirates, Saudi Arabia and Qatar.[18] From Madison Square to Sydney, Suva to Dubai, his words have echoed a singular sentiment. The colour of the passport does not matter. The only thing that is relevant is whether a person is Indian or not. That is enough for him to get help from the Indian government.[19]

Modi sees the diaspora as central to India's development journey and a strategic asset in promoting India's foreign policy interest abroad much in the same way as Jewish diaspora in the USA influences international opinion and policy on Israel. He praises the achievements of Indian diaspora during his visits. He portrays India's image as a victor (power and force to reckon with) and giver in world affairs. The major focus of his diaspora policy has been to tell the world countries that Indians workers are assets to them. PM Modi wants to extend the argument that bilateral relations between that host country and the Indian state are dynamized by this incomparable human resource factor.[20]

Modi Government made a conscious effort to reconnect the Indians living abroad to their homeland by visa regulations and merging the Person of Indian Origin (PIO) and Overseas Citizenship of India (OCI) Card, a single identity card to make it easier for the diaspora to connect with the homeland, secure lifelong Indian visas, avoid checks at local police stations during visits, started a Ministry of Overseas Indian Affairs etc.

Modi's diaspora policy not only focuses on the rich, industrialist, white collared professionals but gives due respect to the working class population. This is evident from the fact that he visited Indian workers camp in Abu Dhabi, starting of Indian Community Welfare Fund (ICWF) to help the Indian community, and also announced an online platform 'MADAD' to assist them. In 2015 the Indian government launched Operation Raahat to evacuate Indian citizens when war broke out in Yemen, Indian workers directly approached the Indian embassy for help. The security and safety of the diaspora has been a top priority. External Affairs Ministry, headed by Sushma Swaraj, has been pro-actively using the social media, especially Twitter, in addressing people's concerns.

Madam Sushma Swaraj, Minister of External Affairs summed up the new government's policy in terms of 3C: inviting diaspora to connect with India, celebrate their cultural heritage and contribute to the development of their homeland.

It is not just the contribution of the diaspora through FDI, remittances and the transfer of knowledge and entrepreneurial means. It is also the positive contribution the diaspora has played in contributing to the rise of the services sector in India, especially in the IT and ITES sectors. Most importantly, the Indian diaspora is also active in local politics in countries like the U.K. and Canada. The government has also urged diaspora members to invest in social projects such as improving rural sanitation and visiting India every year to boost tourism.

A cumulative impact of Modi's diaspora policy is that India retained the top slot among world's largest remittance recipient country in 2015 with $69 billion despite experiencing a $1 billion drop from the previous year. A second consequence of Modi's diaspora policy, albeit indirectly, is tremendous increase in the flow of FDI during last 3 years of Modi rule: from $36 billion in 2013-14 to $60 billion in 2016-17. Moreover, it also helped in giving recognition and respect to Indian diasporic community in the world.

Conclusion

The Indian diaspora is India's valued asset — many of the members are leading various companies and public organisations in different sectors worldwide. Some have become ambassadors, others have headed Governments, many have become an important part of the political systems abroad. The challenge before the Modi Government now is to harness upon this intellectual and economical capital by encouraging the *pravasi* community members to contribute more for their country, as they will always belong here.

Endnotes

1   Rao,Ashok.The Indian Diaspora- Past, Present and Future. Available at: https://www.fairobserver.com/region/central_south_asia/indian-diaspora-past-present-and-future-part-i/ Accessed on 15/10/2017

2   Ibid

3   M, Mahalingam. India's Diaspora Policy and Foreign Policy: An Overview. Available at: http://www.grfdt.com/PublicationDetails. aspx?Type=Articles&TabId=30 accessed on 18/10/2017

4   Ibid

5   Ibid

6   Ibid

7   Chaulia, Shreeram. Modi Doctrine – The Foreign Policy of India's Prime Minister Available at https://www.jgu.edu.in/JGU/news/modi-doctrine-the-foreign-policy-of-india-s-prime-minister-a-book-authored-by-prof-dr-sreeram-chaulia-dean-jsia-is-ranked-amongst-top-10-books-of-the-year-2016 Accessed on 19/10/2017

8   Ibid

9   M, Mahalingam,no.3

10 Ibid

11 Chaulia,No.7

12 M, Mahalingam,no.3

13 For the above paragraph refer to M, Mahalingam,no.3

14 Ibid

15 Ibid

16 Ibid

17 Raja Mohan, C. Narendra Modi and the Diaspora: From the Indian to South Asian Available at http://indianexpress.com/article/blogs/ narendra-modi-and-the-diaspora-from-the-indian-to-south-asian-4464913/ Accessed on 21/10/2017

18 Is India's diaspora policy a double-edged sword? Available at http://www.thehindu.com/thread/politics-and-policy/article17012930.ece

Accessed on 24/10/2017

19 Ibid

20 Chaulia,No.7

Securing the Environment and Promoting Gender Security

VC Shushant Parashar

Abstract

Climate change has become an issue that has garnered as lot of attention on both international and regional spectrums. At the forefront are the poor who will face the initial burnt of climate change as the immediate impact of climate and environmental change will have a direct impact on their livelihood and security. Of the many living below the poverty line, women make up about 70%. It is said that they will the bear the heaviest burden when natural disasters strike. At the same time women are overlooked as potential solution contributors to climate change solutions and thus enabling human security.

The 2005 United Nations Conference on Disaster Reduction has stated the need for a gender perspective in disaster risk management policies and associated decision-making process. It is thus important for governments and policy holders to build policies and programmes that promote the environment and gender security.

The proposed paper aims at presenting a gendered based perspective on how the security of the environment promotes gender security. The paper will also look into whether adequate options exist for women to participate in order to improve human security via environment security in the changing face of climate change.

The study focuses on the effects of climate change on women, who are the most disadvantaged and neglected in the society. Women's contributions to climate change adaptation are also examined as well as related policies.

Keywords: India, Climate Change, Environment, Gender Security, Environmental Security.

Introduction

Environmental change is progressively perceived as a noteworthy human security issue that presents genuine worldwide dangers. For the world's poor the effect will be most serious, lopsidedly influencing their occupation and security. Women are a part of the 70% of those living beneath the poverty line. Hence, they are destined to hold up the heaviest weights when natural disaster's strike. Meanwhile, women are all the more disregarded as potential contributors to the issue of climate change and in this manner to the security of every individual.

The Hyogo Framework for Action that rose up out of the United Nation's 2005 World Meeting on Disaster Reduction expresses the need for a "gender oriented point of view that needs to be integrated into all calamity prevention administration strategies, plans and basic leadership forms, including those identified with chance evaluation, early cautioning, data administration and instruction and preparing"[1]. It is in this way basic that legislature and other partners incorporate within their approaches and projects solid connections between gender, environment security and climate change.

The paper presents a gendered examination of how changes in environmental have a phenomenal impact on the human security. It also surveys whether a satisfactory scope exists for women to take part in improving human security in direct correlation with the changing climate. In light of this examination, proposals have been given for improving the incorporation of a gender perspective in climate change and environmental security policies and projects.

Materials and Methods

The paper is purely based on secondary data sources and consists of data collected from secondary sources that include published works, books, policy briefs, reports, articles from newspapers and magazines be used alongside internet resources to analyse the research problem.

The secondary data source has helped the researcher to understand the issue of environmental security and its importance in relation to gender security. The studies focus on the need to explore environmental security and implications on its implications on gender. It has also come to the notice of scarcity of literature related to the issue at both regional and international level.

Results

Gender, Climate Change and Environmental Security

This part of the paper portrays how climate change, environment and gender security are related. It analyses the impact of climate change on the existing environment and the womenfolk and women's strategies to reinforce human security when climate change occurs. Freedom from threats that interfere with the survival of an individual[2] is called Security. There are different ways to think what security is and sticking to one of these definitions shouldn't be preached. Instead, different perspectives, concepts, institutions and challenges should be exercised as security is a dynamic area because of the global politics, the rise in technology, world-changing events, growing academic interest and allocation of resources that play a vital role in its evolution[3]. Security is as old as the human society and has different connotations depending upon its time and place in human history[4]. Security was and is an essentially contested concept[5]. Initially, security meant protecting the state from external threat. This proposition went on from WWI to WWII. During the Cold War security meant having a nuclear deterrence and the tools to manage a crisis in case one took place.

Post-Cold War, security had a paradigm shift as there arose the need to include areas such as global warming, the rise of epidemic diseases, environmental degradation, integration of markets at a global level and economically underdeveloped parts of the world. Of the many mentioned issues, environmental security is gaining momentum as many of the issues are reversible but that of climate change and it impacts global security in an irreversible manner.

There is disagreement over what constitutes to be part of the environment. Providing an answer to such a simple question is a daunting task as any answer would require an explanation. One could say the environment is a land untouched by human activity but then what about the people that reside within say a forest; secondly are natural environment disasters any different than the disasters caused by man. To come up with a meaning for the term 'Environment' is not worthwhile as it is a dynamic concept. Depending upon where people are, there is a multitude of definitions for the environment. Some see the environment as a resource provider for humans (Anthropocentric)[6] while other's see the environment as being a provider of resource for other living beings as well as the human race (Ecocentric)[7]. This distinction that whether the environment is anthropocentric or ecocentric is directly related to the security of a nation. A link was thus established between security and environment which was further strengthened by the rise of various environmental issues. The dialogue on environmental security revolves around two aspects: (i) security from the environment, (ii) security of the environment. The first one means the security of the human race against threats emanating from the environment while the second means the security of the natural environment from man. Many actors emphasise the need to secure the environment as its degradation has a negative impact on human security, which is an anthropocentric viewpoint, and say there is a need for sustainable development in order to avoid environment and human insecurity. However, many disagree and put forward the point that human behaviour needs to be curtailed in order to prevent environmental degradation and conceptualisation of security needs to take place thus promoting an eco-centric viewpoint, making it clear that humans and the environment are inseparable. In order to safeguard human security, environment security should be the foremost priority of the state as man-made changes to the environment will only threaten the human race and to prevent further damage, sustainable and moderate usage of the environment and its resources is to be promoted on an international scale. The core belief of environmental security is to repair the environment for human life support and prevention of environment degradation from human beings[8].

Discourses on the connection between environment and security have been taking place since the 60's and the 70's. Environmental consciousness grew in both the developing and the developed nations as various publications came to the forefront explaining the ill effects man-made substances have on the environment. The movement gained momentum with the growth of various environment based non-governmental organisations with the aim of creating awareness among the mass, promoting research based on the environment, fund raising etc., to name a few. There was also a surge in various summits whose main theme was environmental issues which led to many international agreements being signed. The academic community has too contributed its fair share in the development of a global environmental security policy by coming up with various publications saying environmental risks should be managed as they are a threat to both national and international security[9]. According to a 1983 article, a threat which hampers with the lives of the people and with the existence of any organisation within a nation-state is to be deemed as a national security threat[10]. Thus if the environment is degraded in any form, the economy of a nation-state will decline thereby creating a tear in the social fabric, hence leading to the disruption of the political structure of the nation-state and conflicts both internally and externally[11].

Literature produced by the academic circle has made environmental security an important concept in security studies. At the start of the 21st century, there is a growing perception which says damage to the environment in harmful to both the environment itself and to human security by impairing access to water, food and other natural resources and impeding their access to other social and economic freedom.

Climate change and Human security

A natural variety in the climate has existed for many centuries: ice ages to tropical/sub-tropical periods have been there throughout earth's history. Be that as it may, anthropogenic environmental change has bit by bit developed since the mechanical revolution, since the 1950's, because of accessibility to petroleum derivatives and the sensational rise in their use[12]. The nature and degree of climatic changes not only delays the process of human advancement and environment protection, yet additionally aids in the development of noteworthy dangers to human security at international, national, regional and livelihood levels[13].

The environmental change also has the ability to start a torrent of conflicts between and within countries, as natural assets are becoming scarcer by the day and various natural disasters can destroy the vocations of the people expanding the number of transients and outcasts.

However, climate change is not only a political and monetary issue. A large portion of it is a human issue where the jobs of many and their security are at stake. Human security undermined and clashes can emerge when an environmental change has an impact on the nourishment, well-being and the ability to gain access to water by an individual. The rise in ocean level will lead to the relocation of communities which in turn can lead to conflict. Nations which are fragile and run the risk of being termed as rogue nations, environmental change will make them more unstable and prone to conflicts.

Natural Disasters and Gender

A significant number of the ramifications caused by climate change on gender have been widely recorded in the existing literature by various authors. Women are frequently more powerless against calamities than men through their socially built parts and obligations and in the light of the fact that they are poorer[14].

By and large, women have less access to assets that are basic in disaster preparedness, relief and recovery. Divisions on the bases of gender frequently results in the over representation of women in fields such as agriculture and informal sectors which are more vulnerable to natural catastrophes. Women, by and large, are additionally in charge of tasks such as food gathering, wood for energy purposes and as well as care giving tasks[15]. Water, sanitation and wellbeing challenges put an extra weight on the women and strains the women's existing productive and reproductive duties when there is a natural disaster and a collapse in business[16].

Gender, Environmental Security and Climate Change in India

To a majority of Indians, natural disasters are a part and parcel of their daily lives. India, on a periodical basis, is affected by drought, floods, cyclones and a plethora of natural disasters. The very existence of the people is threatened with climate change adding fuel to fire. India is seeing the signs of climate change everywhere; from the melting of glaciers to the devastation of farmland due to drought to flood and cyclones, thus challenging the process of development in the country. Disasters taking place due to climate change have already affected the people and the nation alike by reducing economic opportunity and increasing poverty and unemployment, thus making those who are poor to face the brunt of climate change.

India is one of the most populous countries in the world with a population of 1.3 billion people. The majority of natural resources of the country- land, water, forest etc., are gradually decreasing with the ever-increasing demographic pressure. Thus, it can be said that India is in a situation wherein it has a huge population base but not enough resources to sustain them. The situation is further deteriorated by natural disasters routinely occurring. With an over-dependence of the population on the environmental resource base, there is a rapid decline in environmental resources which has led to decrease in agricultural land, loss of habitat for both humans and animals and an increase in health hazards. They, in turn, are causing a number of socio-economic problems which in turn affects the security of the country and the people residing within its borders.

The land is a strategic resource in India and is seen as a symbol of status, plays a vital role in the development of India's economic strategies and is a part of the socio-cultural identity of a nation which is based on agrarian economy[17]. However, in a developing nation such as India, land which is a non-renewable resource, is facing intense pressure which is way beyond its carrying capacity. All economic sectors depend on the available land and with each passing year this dependence is increasing, thus leading to conflict. Conflict over land is varied and ranges from the division of land on the basis of inheritance to owning of land by the government to boundaries between plots to illegal encroachment to territorial dispute from its neighbours like Bangladesh, Pakistan to name a few. The misuse of land has caused its degradation due to which there is a decline in its productivity. Encroachment of forest lands, forest fires, dumping of human and industrial waste, indiscriminate use of fertilisers and other chemicals, improper methods of irrigation etc. are responsible for land degradation in India. Other factors responsible for land wastage include the economic status of agricultural people, poverty, direct access to natural resources and shortage of land etc[18].

Air, next to food and water is an important resource when it comes to human survival on planet earth. It also keeps plants and animals alive. But in recent years, the quality of air in both the world and India is deteriorating due to urbanisation, rise in the number of vehicles and a rapid industrialisation process. Hence the maintenance of air quality in India is a balancing act. Air is being polluted as human activities put substances as sulphur dioxide, nitrogen dioxide, suspended air particulate matter, lead and carbon monoxide etc., in the airs which interfere with the health, property and crop yield[19]. Air pollution is a matter of grave concern in India and according to various reports; the air quality is amongst the worst countries in the world. Deaths due to air pollution are the highest in India. But there is some respite as many of the Indian states are taking various measures to kerb air pollution and thus bring down the mortality rate[20].

Water, like other natural resources, is renewable by nature but is limited in terms of quantity. It is essential for the survival of social communities and nations alike. Water also aids in the maintenance and enhancement of the quality of the environment[21]. Thus access to water is necessary for the survival of the individual and the state. But there is limited availability of freshwater as 70 per cent of the earth's surface is covered with water with much of being saltwater (oceans and seas) and rest being freshwater (rivers and ice at mountains and the poles) of which only a small proportion is available for human consumption[22]. India is blessed with an adequate supply of fresh water resources and accounts for 4 per cent of world's fresh water resources. Yet it seems less due to the rise in population which in turn puts stress on the availability and renewability of freshwater resources. Also, the situation varies from place to place in India as some are drought affected while others are perennially flooded. This causes economic loss to the nation and suffering to the people[23]. Water resources in India are under great duress as many of the natural sources of water are getting polluted and some are on the verge of depletion due to overuse[24]. India is also seeing a rise in the process of development which has further put pressure on the availability of freshwater. Groundwater is being depleted while at the same time rivers, lakes and other water resources on the surface at gradually being polluted, making them unfit for human consumption.

Environmental change is influencing everyone paying little mind to cast, ethnicity, sex, race or the level of the salary. Be that as it may, many women endure due to the fact that they are women and they are poorer. Their unequal position in the public eye implies women have less access to cash, land, and food, protection from savagery, education or medical services. They are more dependent on natural assets for their day to day needs which makes them more exposed to changes in the climate and thus making unable to look after their families.

Women are severely affected by climate change. One of the essential reasons why women are helpless against the impact of climate change is that they excessively dependent on undermined natural resources. As product yields decrease and assets progress towards becoming scarcer, the workload of the women grows thereby endangering their odds to work outside the home or go to school. In times of famine, women are burdened with the task of finding water; refining it and bringing it back in order to look after the needs of the family[25].

As water related illness increment due to environmental change, women bear the additional weight of expanded care giving and expanded dangers to their own health[26]. Pregnant women are especially powerless in the light of the fact that they are prone to intestinal sickness thus making them more vulnerable and fragile to sickness which in turn can lead to high infant mortality rate[27]. Since it is the poor women who are excessively influenced by environmental change, there is a solid case for the need to guarantee that adaptation funds are accessible in order to bolster women's adjustment to environmental change. Climate change interventions that fail to neglect to help those most influenced by climate change and strengthen the dissimilarity among men and women in their ability to adjust to it[28].

According to a report formed by Institute of Development Studies and Action Aid, United Kingdom; women in South Asia especially in countries like India, Nepal and Bangladesh who live near rivers; in the case of the report the Gangetic Plains, were much prone to climate change and its impact. Environmental change has a huge impact on individual's occupations as they are unable to regroup and are unable to get food. In this case, the most impact is felt by the women as they are the primary caregivers for a family. Lose of a source of income leads women down the path of destitution and thereby causes more inequality and marginalisation. Flooding in the Ganga basin is a general occasion as the yearly surges are crucial for recharging the fertility of the soil, aids in the transportation system and make the river grow. Due to climate change, there is a massive change in the recurrence, timing and power of the hazards associated with the floods, thus making it the new reality with which many women living near the river's basin, especially in India, have to accept and cope with. A massive scale of floods and associated hazards cause misfortune of products, domesticated animals and property.

Women have minimal decision as to whether work as a daily wage worker or obtain money from lenders who charge a huge interest rate. Women are affected psychological by various natural disasters caused due to climate change. This also puts a stress on their role as caregivers[29].

Results

Environmental change is a developing human security issue that undermines various groups. The nature and degree of climatic changes not only impedes human advancement and ecological security, yet additionally frames a noteworthy human security danger at national and vocational levels, especially the world's most helpless gatherings. A vulnerability approach is required as various individuals in assorted settings have extraordinary vulnerabilities. Weakness and clashes happen where climate has an impact on the nourishment, water and the accessibility of resources leading to migration. In order to mitigate the risk of climate on human, environment and gender security, the best way is to be prepared for it.

Environmental change is gender neutral. As environmental change has the ability to amplify existing disparities, with gender inequality being a standout amongst the most unavoidable, it has real effects on the women which are unavoidable. Women are probably going to encounter exacerbating imbalance of various sizes as an aftereffect of environmental impacts through their socially built parts, rights and obligations, and in the light of the fact that they are frequently poorer.

Gender differences contrasts must be considered as far as differential powerlessness as well as differential versatile limit. Women assume a key part in securing, overseeing and recuperating their family unit and resources amid a fiasco. They have been solid backers for readiness measures at the group level since they comprehend what catastrophe implies to everyday substances of life. Numerous women have the learning ability to contribute towards adjusting to the changing idea of fiascos and they themselves develop inventive approaches to address as per the demand of the situation. Openings for the women to adapt to calamities today could assume comparative parts in adjusting to environmental change.

More noteworthy consideration of women and incorporation of a gender orientated particular approach are required in order to promote gender, environment and human security.

A lot needs to be done in order to promote gender and environmental security in India. In order to formulate proper adaptation measures in order to mitigate the negative impact of climate change, gender considerations need to be accepted within the adaptation paradigm. Availability of proper funds is a prime requirement as cash available during any natural disaster can give a huge boost to the morale of any affected women thereby decreasing the impact of disaster. Also, disaster funds can't alone mitigate the stress of climate change for poor groups and women. Additionally, empowering strategies and institutional instruments that promote gender equality are of urgent requirement. States and various other foundations need to play an integral role in the management of funds for adaptation purposes. Administration and societal responsibility to gender equality are essential for promoting gender equality. Promotion of equal rights is also a necessity. There needs to be a guarantee of procedural equity when it comes to the outlining and execution of adaptation finance. Interests of the women need to be looked after so that they participate in the process of fund management. Livelihood priorities of the women need to be looked after. States need to promote gender equality in order for the women to cooperate in the disaster management process.

Discussions

Achieving environmental security is of immense importance for not only economic growth but also for the alleviation of poverty and unemployment in order to achieve sustainable development. India is a nation on the path of development and with each step, the requirements increase tenfold.

Development in India is rising. However, with development,

the natural environment is at risk the most. India is also plagued by poverty which co-incidentally requires one to develop more in order to remove it and is also facing external threats when it comes to the environment. Climate change is one and the other being that of China which has set its eyes on building dams in Tibet and is also a growing economic power which in turn further affects the delicate climate of India.

Environmental security and gender security is of great importance for India in the coming future. The field of environmental security holds an important ground as world leaders have recognised its importance and the dangers that will have to be faced if one neglects environmental security. It is, therefore, imperative that India take advantage of the situation and cooperate on a regional and global level to secure the environment and thus promote gender security.

Endnotes

1   (2005). *Hyogo Framework for Action 2005-2015: Building the resilience of nations and communities to disasters*. World Conference on Disaster Reduction.

2   Booth, Ken. (2007). *Theory of World Security*. Cambridge University Press.

3   Buzan, Barry & Hansen, Lene. (2009). *The Evolution of International Security Studies*. Cambridge University Press.

4   Rothschild, Emma. (1995). 'What is security?'.*Daedalus*. 124(3): 53-98.

5   Gallie, W.B.(1956). 'Essentially Contested Concepts'. *Proceedings in the Aristotelian Society*. 56, 167-198.

6   Detraz, Nicole. (2015). *Environmental Security and Gender*. Routledge.

7   Paterson, Mathew. (2001). *Understanding Global Environmental Politics: Domination, Accumulation and Resistance*. Palgrave.

8   Morel, Benoit &Linkov, Igor. (2006). *Environmental security and*

environmental management: the role of risk assessment. Springer.

9 Barnett, Jon. (2007). Environmental Security. in Collins, Alan. (ed.). *Contemporary Security Studies*. Oxford University Press.

10 Ibid, pp: 182-200.

11 Myers, N.(1986).The environmental dimension to security issues. *Environmentalist*. 6(4): 251-257.

12 Adger, Neil & Agarwal, Pramod. (2005). Summary for policy makers. In Parry, M.L. & Hanson, C.E. (eds.). *Climate Change 2007: Impacts, Adaptation and Vulnerability: Contribution of Working Group II to the Fourth Assessment Report of the Intergovernmental Panel on Climate Change.*Cambridge University Press, pp 7-22.

13 Russell, Ben & Morris, Nigel. (2006). Armed forces are put on standby to tackle threat of wars over water. Independent. Retrieved from http://news.independent.co.uk/environment/article348196.ece

14 Mitchell, Tom; Tanner, Thomas &Lussier, Kattie. (2007). *We know what we want: South Asian women speak out on climate change adaption*. Action Aid.

15 Enarson, E. (2000). *Gender and Natural Disasters*. Geneva: International Labour Organisation.

16 Patt, Anthony; Daze, Angie & Suarez, Pablo. (2007). Gender and climate change vulnerability: what's the problem, what's the solution? In M, Ruth & M.E, Ibrarraran. (eds.). *Distributional impacts of climate change and disasters: Concept and Cases*. Edward Edgar Publishing.

17 Chopra, K.(1989). Land Degradation: Dimensions and Casualties. *Indian Journal of Agriculture Economics*. 44(1): 45-53.

18 MoEF.(2009). State of Environment Report India, Environmental Information System (ENVIS), Ministry of Environment and Forest, Government of India.

19 Nagdeve, D.A.(2012). Urban air pollution and its influence on health in India. in Bhagat, R.B.(ed.). *Population, Environment and Health*. Rajat Publications.

20 MoEF.(2009), Ibid.

21 Singh, K.(2009). Environmental degradation and measures for its

mitigation with special reference to India's agriculture sector. *Indian Journal of Agricultural Economics*. 64(1), 40-61.

22 CSE.(2004). It's not agriculture, it's industry. *Down to earth supplement on water use in industry*. Centre for Science and Environment.

23 CSO.(2010).Compendium of environmental statistics. Central Statistical Organisation, Government of India, New Delhi.

24 Singh, K & Shishodia, A.(2007). *Environmental Economics- Theory and Applications*. New Sage Publications.

25 COP 10. (2004). *Mainstreaming gender into the climate change regime*. Buenos Aires.

26 Denton, Fatma. (2004). Gender and Climate change: Giving the "Latecomer" a head start. *IDS Bulletin*. 35(3), pp 42-49.

27 Mitchell, Tom; Tanner, Thomas &Lussier, Kattie. (2007). *We know what we want: South Asian women speak out on climate change adaption*. Action Aid.

28 Denton, Fatma. (2004). Gender and Climate change: Giving the "Latecomer" a head start. *IDS Bulletin*. 35(3), pp 42-49.

29 Mitchell, Tom; Tanner, Thomas & Lussier, Kattie. (2007). *We know what we want: South Asian women speak out on climate change adaption*. Action Aid.

Social Welfare Measures in Contemporary Indian Polity

Dr. Nandini Sahay

Our country is one of the largest democracies in the world and it is considered to be a welfare state where the citizen's welfare is the priority. As per our Constitution, the sovereignty vests in the people of the country. Keeping this aspect in mind, the present Government under the leadership of Shri Narendra Modi has initiated many social welfare schemes and programmes which will carter to the needs of the weaker sections of the society including women, children, handicapped, aged, Scheduled Castes & Scheduled Tribes etc. Women and children constitute around 70% of our country's population. A nation cannot develop if they are not taken care of. Therefore, the present Government's social welfare schemes aim to make programmes and schemes more efficient and give priority to the empowerment of the vulnerable section of the society including women and children.

Some of the social welfare Schemes launched by the present Government are briefly discussed as under :

One Stop Centre[1]

Social problems like child marriage, rape, dowry, acid attacks, honour killings, domestic violence, sexual abuse, trafficking of girl child for sexual exploitation, child labour, female foeticide etc., affect the rights of women. Apart from these social issues, India is struggling with violence due to the lower status of women, particularly in times of displacement and communal riots.

The 12th Plan Working Group on Women's Empowerment suggested to set up One Stop Crisis Centres on a pilot basis, for providing shelter, police assistance, legal, medical and counselling services to women who are the victims of violence with the help of a Helpline which is available 24 hours a day. This One Stop Centre, which is also known as Sakhi Centres is set up by the government of India. The scheme began to function across India from April 2015.

Ujjawala[2]

Trafficking of women and children affect their basic human rights. Lower status of women, poverty, lack of proper implementation of laws etc. are some of the reasons for trafficking in India. To solve this problem, government has formulated and introduced a Central Scheme "Comprehensive Scheme for Prevention of Trafficking for Rescue, Rehabilitation and Re-Integration of Victims of Trafficking for Commercial Sexual Exploitation-Ujjawala". The aim of the Scheme is to prevent trafficking of women and children for commercial sexual exploitation through social mobilization and involvement of local communities, awareness generation programmes, generation of public opinion through workshops/ seminars and other similar activity. Victims would also be rescued from the place of their exploitation. Further rehabilitation services would be provided to the victims. Their basic need such as food, shelter, clothing, health checkup would be taken care of. They would also be provided vocational training so that they can become independent. An effort would also be made to reintegrate victims into the family and society and repatriate cross bordered victims to their country of origin.

Beti Bachao Beti Padhao Scheme (BBBP)[3]

As per the Census (2011), Child Sex Ratio showed an alarming declining trend. It was 918 in 2011 compared to 976 in 1961. This is an indicator of women lacking empowerment. Alarmed by the sharp decline, the Government of India introduced *Beti Bachao, Beti Padhao* (BBBP) scheme. The Scheme was launched in January 2015 by Prime Minister Sri Narendra Modi at Panipat in Haryana. The scheme aims at promoting gender equality and significance of educating girls. It is a social campaign that aims to generate awareness and improve the efficiency of welfare services meant for girls. The main objective of this programme is to improve the Child Sex Ratio (CSR) by promoting girls' education, preventing gender-biased sex selection by enforcing PC&PNDT Act and promoting empowerment of women at all the stages of life.

Mahila E-Haat[4]

Mahila E-Haat, is a bilingual portal which was launched by the Ministry of Women & Child Development on 7th March, 2016. It is an online marketing platform leveraging technology for supporting women entrepreneurs/SHGs/NGOs for showcasing the products/services which are made/manufactured/undertaken by them. It is an initiative for meeting aspirations and fulfilling needs of women.

Technology is a critical component for enhancing efficiency in business of women entrepreneurs / SHGs / NGOs. This portal would provide a special marketing platform for women. The aim of this portal is the financial inclusion and economic empowerment of women. This e-platform will showcase the products and services. To avail the benefit of this programme, women need to be majorly involved in the value chain. The vendors will be allowed to price their products and charge accordingly from the buyers. It is a web-based programme which has unlimited reach. To increase it's visibility, major PSUs, IRCTC, Nationalised Banks like SBI have given a link to Mahila E -haat on their websites to make it simple to join Mahila E-haat. Sensitization, advocacy, training and soft intervention workshops on Mahila E-haat are organized periodically with the support of State Governments & Women Development Corporations.

Mahila Coir Yojana (MCY)[5]

A self employment generation programme named Mahila Coir Yojana (MCY) was introduced to provide self-employment to rural women artisans in regions where coir fibre is produced. The scheme is running in coir producing coastal States such as Kerala, Tamil Nadu, Karnataka, Andhra Pradesh, Telangana, Odisha, Lakshadweep, Maharashtra, Gujarat, Goa, Puducherry, A& N Islands, West Bengal and NE Region. Only one artisan per household would be eligible to receive assistance under the scheme.

Pradhan Mantri Matru Vandana Yojana[6]

Women in India lack nutrition and are also anaemic. A mother who is undernourished will inevitably give birth to a low birth weight baby. Women from lower economic strata have to work till the last day of pregnancy to earn a living for their family. Furthermore, they go back to their work soon after the childbirth which might harm them. The objective of this initiative of the government is to provide compensation for the loss of income in terms of cash incentives. This would help women take care of themselves pre and post-delivery of the first child. The cash incentive provided under this scheme would lead to improved health of Pregnant Women and Lactating Mothers (PW& LM). Women who had case of miscarriage and still birth, will also get benefit from this scheme. This scheme would provide cash incentive of Rs 5000 in three instalments.

> ➢ First instalment of Rs 1000/ - on early registration of pregnancy at the Anganwadi Centre (AWC) / approved Health facility as may be identified by the respective administering State / UT.

> ➢ Second instalment of Rs 2000/ - after six months of pregnancy on receiving at least one ante-natal check-up (ANC)

> ➢ Third instalment of Rs 2000/ - after child birth is registered and the child has received the first cycle of BCG, OPV, DPT and Hepatitis - B, or its equivalent/ substitute.

The eligible beneficiaries would receive the incentive given under the Janani Suraksha Yojana (JSY) for institutional delivery and the incentive received under JSY would be accounted towards maternity benefits so that on an average a woman gets Rs 6000/-

Pradhan Mantri Ujjwala Yojana (PMUY)[7]

Pradhan Mantri Ujjwala Yojana was introduced on 01/05/2016 in Ballia, Uttar Pradesh and subsequently, the scheme was launched on 15/05/2016 in Dahod (Gujarat). The aim of the programme is to provide free LPG connection with financial assistance of Rs. 1600/- per connection to an adult woman member of BPL family. This LPG connection will be given to women member of BPL house hold who suffer from at least one deprivation as per SECC 2011 (Rural) data. The charges of Rs 1600 will be reimbursed by the Government of India.

Pradhan Mantri LPG Subsidy PAHAL Yojana (DBTL)[8]

The full form of PAHAL Yojana is Pratyaksh Hanstantarit Scheme and concerns the LPG customers. This scheme was initially launched in 54 districts of India. Later, the scheme was introduced in the whole country. The objective is to remove leakages, prevent black-marketing in cash subsidy on cooking gas. This scheme would make every consumer eligible for a subsidy. The subsidy that a consumer gets under this scheme would be directly transferred to the customer's bank account."Direct Benefit Transfer on LPG (DBTL)" scheme has become the world's largest direct benefit transfer scheme after 2.5 crore households received about 550 crore rupees since 15th November 2014. This scheme directly facilitates cash subsidy on cooking gas to go to consumers so that they are able to buy cooking gas at market price.

Social Security Schemes[9]

On 9th May, 2015 Prime Minister Narendra Modi launched three mega social security schemes in Kolkata, to widen the process of financial inclusion in the country, which are given below:

> Atal Pension Yojana (APY).

> Pradhan Mantri Jeevan Jyoti Yojana (PMJJBY).

> Pradhan Mantri Suraksha BimaYojana (PMSBY).

Atal Pension Yojana (APY)

Under APY scheme, the pension subscribers will receive a fixed minimum monthly pension ranging from 1,000 rupees to 5,000 rupees at the age of 60. To avail the benefit of this scheme, the beneficiary should have a bank account and should not be a member of any statutory body. This is a social security scheme. The aim of this scheme is to provide security to people who are working in an unorganised sector. The Pension Fund Regulatory and Development Authority (PFRDA) would administer the whole process.

Pradhan Mantri Jeevan Jyoti Yojana (PMJJBY)

Under this scheme, the beneficiary who is the insurance subscriber, will get an annual life insurance in case of death. A person should have a bank account. Rs2 Lakh rupees would be given in case of death.

Pradhan Mantri Suraksha Bima Yojana (PMSBY)

Under this scheme, the beneficiary who is the insurance subscriber will get annual life insurance in case of accidental death, partial disability or full disability. He/she should be in the age group of 18 to 70 years. The person must have Aadhaar number linked to the bank account.

Pradhan Mantri Surakshit Matritva Abhiyan (PMSMA)[10]

Pradhan Mantri Surakshit Matritva Abhiyan Scheme was launched by Hon'ble Prime Minister on 9th June, 2016. The aim is to improve the quality and coverage of Antenatal Care (ANC) including diagnostics and counselling services as part of the Reproductive Maternal Neonatal Child and Adolescent Health (RMNCH+A) Strategy. It is an initiative of the Ministry of Health & Family Welfare (MoHFW), Government of India. The scheme provides comprehensive and quality antenatal care which would be free of cost and universal to all pregnant women. Under this scheme, antenatal care services would be provided to women in their 2nd/3rd trimesters of pregnancy in government hospitals.

The programme also intends to engage the private sector. This includes motivating private practitioners to volunteer for the campaign developing strategies for generating awareness and appealing to the private sector to participate in the initiative at government health facilities. The aim is to ensure at least one antenatal checkup for all pregnant women in their second or third trimester by a physician/specialist and improve the quality of care during ante-natal visits.

Pradhan Mantri Kaushal VikasYojana (PMKVY)[11]

Pradhan Mantri Kaushal Vikas Yojana (PMKVY), India's largest Skill Certification Scheme, was launched on 15 July, 2015 on the occasion of World Youth Skills Dayto skill youth, including class 10 and 12 drop outs.

It would be also associated with Union Government's flagship programmes such as Make in India, Digital India and Swachh Bharat Abhiyan. Soft skills, good work ethics, personal grooming, behavioural change for cleanliness etc.are also a part of the training programme. A sum of 1,500 crore rupees has been allotted for this scheme.

Stand Up India Scheme for women and SC/ST[12]

Prime Minister Narendra Modi launched the Stand-up India scheme aimed at providing credit to Scheduled Caste (SC), Scheduled Tribe (ST), and women borrowers in the non-farm sector. The objective is to promote entrepreneurship among SC/ST and women and further give a push to government's financial inclusion programme. A loan between *10 lakh rupees and up to 1 crore rupees* would be provided to SC/ST and women. A Web Portal for online registration and support services will also be provided. Under the scheme, 1.25 lakh bank branches will provide loans up to 1 crore rupees to SC/ST and women entrepreneurs. Thus it will help in creating 2.5 lakh entrepreneurs throughout the country. Stand-up India is a part of *Start-up India*.

Sardar Patel Urban Housing Mission: Housing for all by 2022[13]

Sardar Patel Urban Housing Mission scheme is introduced to build 30 million houses by 2022 for people who are from lower economic strata. Rs 4000 crore has been allocated for scheme by NDA government. The objective of this mission is to build 30 million houses by 2022, for people who are economically weak. *"Har Parivar ko Ghar"* (a house for every family) is the slogan and direction behind this mission. It will be in partnership with private sector. The aim of the mission is to make India a slum-free nation and promote social inclusion of the vulnerable population.

Right to Light Scheme

National Programme for LED-based Home and Street Lighting for energy conservation, for reducing energy consumption, was launched by Prime Minister Narendra Modi. Light Emitting Diode (LED) bulb distribution under the Domestic Efficient Lighting Programme (DELP) and a web-based system to enable consumers in Delhi to register requests for procuring LED bulbs under DELP, was also launched along with this programme. LED bulbs have a very long life, almost 50 times more than ordinary bulbs, and 8-10 times that of CFLs, and therefore provide both energy and cost savings in the medium term. This would save energy worth around 24 crore units every year.

Ek Bharat Shreshtha Bharat[14]

Prime Minister Shri Narendra Modi announced a new programme **'EK Bharat Shreshtha Bharat'**. The aim of this programme is to give a boost to the existing cultural connect between different parts of the country and enhance interaction between people living in different states. The program is inspired by the ideologies of Shree Vallabhbhai Patel who had played an important role in country's freedom fight. A special committee has been constituted to look after this program and related issues. Students are the main participants in this program who need to travel from their own state to the chosen state to learn and exchange the culture and language. This initiative will help them to understand the life and culture of people more closely than before.

NDA government has launched many promising schemes and programmes. The challenge lies in the proper implementation, execution and monitoring of these programmes. Persuasion, motivation, incentives and punishment are the measures which should be used by the government agencies for their employees to make these initiatives of the government successful. Public and private partnership together can make the fruits of the programme reach each needy vulnerable groups and make a positive change in their life.

References

Books and Journals

Dubey, S.N., Administration of Social Welfare Programmes in India, Somaiya Publications, (Bombay), 1973.

JainendraKunmar Das., (Ed) Encyclopedia of Social Series, Social Welfare and Social Work, Anmol PublicaationsPvt. Ltd., (New Delhi), 2002.

Jalan, Jyotsna &Ravallion, Martin, 2003. "Does piped water reduce diarrhea for children in rural India?," Journal of Econometrics, Elsevier, vol. 112(1), pages 153-173, January.

Jha, Raghbendra& Bhattacharyya, Sambit&Gaiha, Raghav& Shankar, Shylashri, 2009. ""Capture" of anti-poverty programs: An analysis of the National Rural Employment Guarantee Program in India," Journal of Asian Economics, Elsevier, vol. 20(4), pages 456-464, September.

KumariShantha., Scheduled Castes and Welfare Measures, Classical Publishing Company, (New Delhi), 1989.

Parvathamma, C., Scheduled Castes and Tribes : A Socio-Economic Survey, Ashish Publishing House, (New Delhi), 1984

Raghbendra Jha & Sambit Bhattacharyya & Raghav Gaiha & Shylashri Shankar, 2008. "Capture of Anti-Poverty Programs: An Analysis of the National Rural Employment Guarantee Program in India," ASARC Working Papers 2008-07, The Australian National University, Australia South Asia Research Centre.

Saksena, R.N. Social Research and Social Welfare In India—Base For an Inter-Disciplinary Approach, *Sociological Bulletin*, Vol. 23, No. 2 (September 1974), pp. 193-20

Singh, R.S., Encyclopaedia of Social Work and Social Welfare in 21st Century, Century Press, (New Delhi), 2010.

Journals and Periodicals

Kurukshetra

Yojana

India - Year Books Mainstream

Manorama - Year Books

Indian Journal ofPublic Administration

Economic and Political Weekly

Dailies

Deccan Chronicle (English)

The Hindu (English)

Times of India (English)

Internet Sources

delhi.gov.in/wps/wcm/connect/doit_socialwelfare/Social Welfare+New/Home/http://planningcommission.nic.in/plans/planrel/fiveyr/1st/1planch36.html

"Government Schemes in India". SarkariJankari. 2014-12-31

"Ministry of urban housing and poverty alleviation scheme"

Ministry of Women and Child Development, GOI -http://www. wcd.nic.in/schemes/one-stop-centre-scheme-1

Ministry of Women and Child Development, GOI   http:// www.wcd.nic.in/schemes/ujjawala-comprehensive-scheme-prevention-trafficking-and-rescue-rehabilitation-and-re

Ministry of Women and Child Development, GOI (http://wcd.nic. in/BBBPScheme/main.htm

Ministry of Micro, Small & Medium Enterprises, GOI, www. msme.nic.in/.../Impact-Mahila-Coir-Yojana-Sche

Ministry of Women & Child, GOI, http://wcd.nic.in/schemes/ pradhan-mantri-matru-vandana-yojana

"National Rural Livelihood Mission: Understanding the vulnerability of low-income groups – Moneylife"

"Press Information Bureau". Pib.nic.in.

"Welcome to Ministry of Rural Development (Govt. of India)". Rural.nic.in.

"Rs. 20,000-crore budget for Namami Gange scheme". The Hindu. 2015-05-13.

socialjustice.nic.in/

Endnotes

1 Ministry of Women and Child Development, GOI -http://www.wcd. nic.in/schemes/one-stop-centre-scheme-1

2 Ministry of Women and Child Development, GOI   http://www. wcd.nic.in/schemes/ujjawala-comprehensive-scheme-prevention-trafficking-and-rescue-rehabilitation-and-re

3 Ministry of Women and Child Development, GOI (http://wcd.nic.in/ BBBPScheme/main.htm

4 Ministry of Women and Child Development, GOI (http://mahilaehaat-rmk. gov.in/en/

5 Ministry of Micro, Small & Medium Enterprises, GOI, www.msme.nic.in/.../

Impact-Mahila-Coir-Yojana-Sche

6 Ministry of Women & Child, GOI, http://wcd.nic.in/schemes/
   pradhan-mantri-matru-vandana-yojana

7 Ministry of Petroleum and Natural Gas, GOI, https:/indane.co.in/
   pradhan-mantri-ujjwala-yojana.php

8 Ministry of Petroleum and Natural Gas, GOI (http://petroleum.nic.in/
   dbt/whatisdbtl.html

9 Ministry of Finance, GOI, http://www.jansuraksha.gov.in/)

10 Ministry of Women & Child Development, GOI https://pmsma.nhp.
    gov.in/about-scheme/

11 Ministry of Skill Development &Entrepreneurship,GOI, http://www.
    pmkvyofficial.org/ Index.aspx

12 Govt. of India, https://www.standupmitra.in/Home/SUISchemes]

13 Ministry of Housing and Urban Poverty Alleviation, GOI

14 https://www.mygov.in/task/ek-bharat-shreshtha-bharat-contest/

Rethinking Indian Federalism: Issues and Challenges

Dr. Suresh Chandra Patel

Introduction

Federalism in India during the last 70 years had passed through two phases. The first phase is a period of centralized federalism and the second one can be called a period of cooperative and competitive federalism. The first phase resulted in strong central dominance due to unitary features of the Indian Constitution and the policy of planned development. As a result, we witnessed subordination of the State to the Centre. But after 1967, with the decline of the Congress Party and the emergence of coalition politics, the second phase started which resulted in a shift in the Centre-States power balance, so much so that the negative results came to the forefront. These negative results were in the form of river-disputes, the creation of new States, Centre-States conflict, etc and all of them led to manifestations of Secessionist movements, strikes regional imbalance etc. This has created problems for the Indian Political System. Desirable reforms are much needed and it is in the context of rethinking Indian federalism in relevant and must be undertaken. It is more so at a time when the importance of 'thinking federalism 'is mounting in different society for appropriate movement and accommodation. The success of Indian democracy can be attributed to 'federalism'. If India wants to become a superpower and play an important role in world politics then its democracy and federalism must continue. This could be possible through a rethinking of Indian federalism.

Federalism in India is a widely debated and discussed matter. Federalism in India and its adoption was conceived as a necessity to meet out exigencies out of the plurality of Indian situation. Indian Federalism is passing through its structural and functional aspects. The growth of regional political parties and the changing perspective of Indian federalism in an important matter for discussion. This paper will focus on the theoretical framework of federalism in India. It will also look into the evolution. This paper will analyze the working of the federalism in India service since its inception. This paper will also analyze the weaknesses in the successful working of Indian federalism and will include certain suggestions in this regard.

The government can be Federal or unitary on the basis of concentration and distribution of power. If there is distribution of power, it is an example of unitary form of Govt. and if there is distribution of power, it is an example of federal form of Govt. federalism is a form of government and a way of life in the Indian Political system In fact, Federalism is gaining increasing acceptance all over the world. Federalism, as a political idea has become increasingly important as a way of reconciling unity and diversity within a political system. The reason for this can be found in the changing nature of the world leading to pressure both for larger states and also for the small states. The term 'Federalism' implies a political system where the Central Government and the constituent States Jointly share the power of the government within their respective Jurisdictions distributed between them under the supreme authority of the constitution. Federalism is a pragmatic political arrangement which aims at maintaining a compromise between the States which wish to come together under the authority of the union and at the same time retain their autonomy and identity. There has been tremendous interest in federalism internationally during the last few decades. Intellectuals, Journalists, Political Leaders etc. are now increasingly talking of federalism as a healthy, liberating positive form of organization. Moreover, countries like Belgium, Spain, South Africa, Ethiopia, Italy and the U.K. appear to be emerging towards new and innovative federal forms. Some other countries of the World are in the process of at least including some features of federalism, if not all, in their system. Thus, federalism continues to gain prominence throughout the world with the change of world situations. Accordingly, the importance of India federalism in the present-day context needs no exaggeration.

India today is an example of a successful federal system in the World. India provides an example of a federalism which has become a highly flexible instrument that can be continuously adapted to new needs and demands. It is also understood as a balance between over-centralization and autonomy of States. Indian federalism is also conducive to the social structure of India which has a plural and multicultural socio-culture cleavages. That is more or less spread across the land from the Himalayas to the Oceans. Prof Iqbal Narain, once pointed out that, Indian federalism is a paradox, a political phenomenon which has not been studied adequately. The framers of the Constitution of India wanted to establish a federal system in view of the social diversities and large size of the country. The primary aim was to form a federation which will provide self-rule at the regional level and shared rule at the federal level." India has adopted a parliamentary form of Govt. within a federal framework. Federal system and its govt. enjoys much more power than its constituent units. Conflicts between the Centre and the States are frequent regarding the distribution of social, economic and cultural power. India has to play a very important role in the world politics. The time has come for India to reflect and review the idea of federalism and strike a fine tuning between the Centre and the States. The current burning issues like Cauvery River Disputes between Tamil Nadu and Karnataka and Mahanadi River Dispute between Odisha and Chhattisgarh, highlight the importance of a rethinking on Indian Federalism. If Indian democracy has to survive and play an important role in the 21st century then its federalism must continue. Hence, there is an urgent need for rethinking Indian federalism and to address is weak points and thereby strengthening it.

Definitions, Meanings & Features

The term "federalism" occupies an important plea in the world politics. The word "federalism" has been derived from the Latin word 'foetus' which literally means a covenant, agreement or a treaty. This Latin word suggests an idea of a promise, commitment and undertaking and therefore the federal idea involves cooperation, reciprocity and mutuality, friendship or faith in one another that political communities express when they decide to join together in a federalism or federal form of Govt. In simple words, federalism can be defined as "a form of organization suited to the communities with a diversified pattern of objectives, interests and traditions who seek to join together in the pursuits of common objectives and interests and the cultivation of common traditions." Here it is noteworthy that the classical definition of federalism has undergone a change due to the new development in the world and global economy and new thoughts. The classical federalism in the world is the result of either Centre petal or centrifugal process. Centrifugal is where federalism has been imposed on the constituent units for managerial convenience and thereby the centre is more dominant and decisive in relation to the constituent units. Centrifugal is where the constituents units take initiatives for forming a federation. Best examples are Canada and Australia. Indian federalism seems to be nearer to that of Canada, Australia. U.S.A, Canada, Switzerland, Australia, Brazil, Argentina etc are the best and prominent example of a federal system of Govt.

India is one of the prominent countries in Asia to adopt a federal system. Indian federalism is about 70 years old. It has served extremely well for India to promote our democracy, to strengthen our national unity and to achieve economic progress. The important features of the Indian federalism are what India calls it "Cooperative federalism." Flexibility is one of the hallmarks of Indian federalism and it has helped in strengthening Indian democracy.

The Constituent Assembly of India provided the soundest frame work for Indian constitution in the form of a federation. Indian federal system is a unique system in its origin, structure and functioning. It is surprising that the term 'federation' or 'federalism' has not been used. Rather the phrase 'union of states' has been preferred under Art-I which provides "India, that is

Bharat, shall be a union of States."

According to K.C. Wheare, "federalism is a system of government in which authority is divided between national and regional governments so that each remains within a sphere, coordinate (i.e. Legally co-equal) and independent."

According to Carl J. Friedrich, "Federalism is a set of Political communities that co-exist and interact as autonomous entities, United in common with an autonomy for its own."

According to W. S. Livingstone, "Federalism is a device by which the articulated and protected."

Thus, federalism is a political system where there are two sets of Governments having a constitutional distribution of powers between them and a strong, interacted judicial system to solve disputes among them, if any.

In other words, the elements of a federal form of government are –

➢ Dual Polity.

➢ Written and rigid constitution.

➢ Constitutional Distribution of powers.

➢ Strong, integrated and independent Judicial system.

Federalism in India has been a part of day to day activities of the society in India. But after 1990, it has become very important with the emergence of coalition era at Centre.

Indian Federalism in Practice

Indian federalism has both empirical and theoretical aspects. It is a dynamic theory of nation-building and state-building. Federalism in India is a grand decision of Living together in the matrix arrangement of what Daniel Elazar conceptually termed as "self-rule plus shared-rule". According to Rasheeduddin Khan, the main objectives of federalism are "unity of policy and plurality of society." As a theory of nation-building, federalism defines state and society relationship in a way which allows identity to different social groups. It is very close to multiculturalism. As a theory of State building, Indian federalism has three essential components.

> Formation of states in such a manner so as to protect and promote closer contact between people and the Govt.

> Distribution of powers on a non-centralized basis.

> Creation of Institution of shared rule.

Granville Austin described the Indian federalism as a cooperative federalism. He observed "cooperative federalism produces a strong Central or General Govt., yet it does not necessarily result in weak provisional governments that is largely administrative agencies for central policies.

Weaknesses

Indian federalism has its own weaknesses. These weaknesses are either inherent or circumstantial. The following weaknesses necessities a rethinking of Indian federalism.

> Unequal allocation of financial resources between the Centre and the States.

> Regionalism leading to demand for a statehood or different areas, state autonomy and emphasis of regional interests over national interests.

> Emergence of coalition Govt. in Indian Political system.

> Federalism leads to lack of uniformity of laws and policies for the whole country.

> Method of distribution of powers in the Indian Political system cannot be perfect for all times.

> Creation of problems by the operation of multi-party system in the Indian Federal system.

> Abuse of the Provision of Art-356.

> Lack of strong national leader.

> Specific and practical problems like illiteracy and poverty, linguistic differences, religious differences etc.

The above are some of the weaknesses of Indian federalism. They lead to the development of confliction and confrontational character. The objective of cooperative federalism has suffered a setback.

The need for Rethinking federalism in India is a legitimate one at a time of widespread discontentment, chaos, increasing demand for state autonomy and growth of political participation in the country. Decentralization of powers and minimum governance, maximum liberty for its citizens and efficient local resources management are the main motives behind the reorganization of states. These objectives are to be effectively tackled to have a perfect federalism in India. Politics of India has also changed. It has become regional in nature. Regional political parties have grown enormously and their growth has severely affected the functioning of the Indian Political system. The Central Govt. is under tremendous pressure. The dominance of the Central Govt. under Indian Federalism has a negative impact on the functioning of the democratic institutions as a whole. This unhealthy trend needs to be checked if Indian federalism is to become successful. The regional imbalance has led to a demand for regional autonomy. The time has come to have a relook into the operation of Indian Federalism.

The makers of the Indian Constitution went for a strong Central Govt. in a quasi-federal political set-up. The primary objectives of this was to prevent further disintegration. This was quite natural on the background of partition after independence. But the problems which they wanted to avoid are still there and continues to plague the Indian federalism. In fact, the Constituent Assembly devised a system according to the then needs of the time and the requirements of a federal society. The framework adopted was very much different from all existing models of federalism. Different ideas were borrowed from different federalism. As a result, the system becomes a new model often described by the Jurists as "quasi-federal". The result was a hybrid federalism of the genus of federalism in which we witness the peculiar combination of self-rule and shared rule. Fortunately, this has worked for Indian federalism. The Constituent Assembly created an "Indestructible union of Destructible States". The strong centre framework has proved to be conducive to the diversities and cleavages of Indian democracy. This is equally true in the age of Globalisation, Liberalisation and Privatisation. The needs for rules and regulations by a strong Centre has emerged in new areas. Even the strongest advocate of state autonomy does not challenge the need for a strong centre.

Indian federalism has become a asymmetric federalism. Unequal States and regions lead to the generation of tensions and dissatisfactions. The Central Govt. has tried to address these problems by granting special status provision, special financial allocation and incentives etc.

The Provision of special status has been used to resolve issues arising from history, geography and culture. The best example is Art-370, another development of Indian federalism which needs rethinking in the growth of Executive Federalism. This refers to the growth of All India Services and their contributions to the growth of Indian federalism. Another development which necessitates rethinking in multi-level federalism and local self-government is the 73rd Constitutional Amendment (1992) which came into operation in 1995 gave Constitutional recognition to a third tier of the federal structure. We have multi-level federalism. The growth of the Panchayati Raj system is an important development of the federal system. There are pressures generated at this level and pressures may pressurize to go for further changes in the institutional design.

Solution

The Indian Federalism has successfully met many challenges since its beginning. The strong points of Indian federalism are a strong centre, flexibility and cooperation among the Centre and the States. Federalism seeks to maintain local identity against national policies. Leading to regionalism. Regionalism is a threat to Indian federalism. There must be a perfect balance between the centre and the states to prevent the growth of regionalism. The Centre should do everything possible to get the co-operation of the states through discussion, persuasion and compromises. It should not resort to showing off its powers except only in case of demonstrable necessity. Federalism is a dynamic and not a static concept. Many problems of Indian Federalism can be solved if Centre and the States pull together.

Indian Federalism: Need for Rethinking

The nature of Indian federalism is one of the most controversial questions about the constitution of India. The native of the federal system in India is very complex. The views of political scientists vary from calling it a federal to a quasi-federal on one hand and unitary with federal features on the other. This diversity of views about the nature of the Indian constitution shows that it has both unitary as well as federal features. This is so because the word federalism appeared nowhere in the Indian Constitution. Instead, Article I of the Constitution provides that "India shall be a Union of States". This is an ambiguity. This has resulted in tensions, debates, conflicts and controversies. Moreover, it reminds us of a mixed Political heritage and reveals the hopes and aspirations of the founding fathers. The problem has been further aggravated by the overall changes in the political process and consequences of socio-economic developments. There is an increasing emphasis on the need to further strengthen the centre. Also, there is a growing demand for state autonomy. It appears that both the demands have been voiced with ulterior motives.

The views of political scientists, as well as the Jurist widely, differ on this question. Paul H. Appleby, Dr. Rajendra Prasad, Pandit Jawaharlal Nehru, T.T. Krishnamachari and many others including Jyoti Basu have described it as federal whereas Dr. K.M. Munshi, Dr. Gajendragadkar and P.S. Deshmukh think that it is more unitary than federal.

The truth lies somewhere between the two Dr. B.R. Amebedkar described it as both unitary as well as federal according to requirement of time and circumstances. It is federal in normal time and unitary in times of war. K.C. Wheare described Indian

Constitution as "quasi-federal". Sir, Ivor Jennings described the Indian Constitution as being federal "with a strong centralizing tendency." Some of the federal features of the Indian constitution are the provisions of dual polity, constitutional distribution of powers, the existence or an independent judiciary, written and rigid constitution, etc. But it cannot be denied that there is a theme of subordination of the states running right through the constitution. The framers of the Indian Constitution were in favour of a strong and united India. It was necessary to deal with fissiparous forces and other parochial tendencies, and also to undertake the tasks of national defence, planning, removal of poverty and backwardness, consolidation of democracy and freedom and performing an affective role in world affairs. At the same time, there was a sincere desire for a federal spirit. That was the constitution and the intent. But the reality today is very different. Even after seventy years of independence, there are many flaws and weaknesses at the structural and functional levels. Since the adoption of the constitution, the trend has been towards amassing of power by the centre, crippling the autonomy of the states. After 1967, political parties with different ideologies captured power. This led to a problem. People's desire for a socio-economic development and change remains unfulfilled. The process of centralization resulted in two interrelated phenomenon i.e. tension in centre-state relations leading to amend for the autonomy of the state and regionalism. The major areas of tensions in Indian federalism are:

Challenges

> ➤ Role of Governor as a representative of the Centre Govt.

> ➤ Misuse of powers of the imposition of President's Rule under Article 356.

> ➤ Reservation of Bills by the consideration of the President under Article 201.

> ➤ Sharing of finances and approval of state project by the centre.

> ➤ Use of Electronic media.

Thus, in India, the Central Government has a dominant position. The question is not whether there should be a strong centre.

The time has come for India and Indians to reflects and review the ideas of federalism and expose the possibility of a better balance between the centre and states. The need for rethinking is clear from the fact that different political scientists describe it differently some describe it as 'federal in form but unitary in spirit,' and another describe it as only "quasi-federal". The Telangana case reflects the necessity of a federal balance and the way states have been created in India in the past Indian federalism needs rethinking more so because of the following contradictions.

> States have no role to play in the creation of new State or States or even in their abolition, were that to happen. The view of the affected state is considered but there is no obligation to action it.

> There is no fixed criteria on the basis of which new State should be created. Administrative efficiency, economic development, language were the criteria in the beginning. But in case of Telangana, history, a distinct identity and economic needs have been preferred.

> There is an incentive for every linguistics, religious and ethnic identity to demand Statehood.

Conclusion

An analysis of the functioning of the Indian federalism reveals that there is an urgent need for proper assessment of Indian federalism. This is more so because of the socio, economic and political changes that have taken place in the new millennium. The structure and functions of the Indian federalism needs to be restructured. Proper amendments of the constitution are required on the needs of the society and in the structure and functions of Indian federalism. Demand for statehood or state autonomy are the major obstacles in the way of Indian federalism. As far as state autonomy is concerned, we may take the help of K. Santhanam.

According to him, "the main purpose of Indian federal system is that when the conditions, the traditions, the circumstances, the climate, the geography differ there should be state autonomy." Moreover, an accommodative approach to solve all these problems is very much needed economic grievances of the State should be taken seriously and adequate financial assistance should be given to the States. Central bureaucracy should be reduced. A constructive approach to the study of Indian federalism is needed. River disputes like Mahanadi, Godavari, Narmada, Cauvery should be solved immediately. There must be a co-operative federalism. Above all, a political well is needed to make the federation a reality one. These are some facts which require immediate rethinking.

References

Chakraborty, Bidyut (1999) The Changing Contours of Federalism in India And Strains (Delhi: Macmillan).

Where, K.C. (1963) Federal Government (London: Oxford University Press).

Aiyar, S.P., (1961) Federalism and Social Change (Bombay: Asian Publishing House).

Austin, Granville, (1966) The Indian Constitution: Cornerstone Of A Nation (Oxford: Clarendon Press).

Bakhru, Mitra, (1988) Dynamics of Federal Bargaining, (New Delhi Intellectual Publishing House).

Bobmwall, K.R. (1967) The Foundation of Indian Federalism (Delhi: Asia Publishing House)

Basu, D.D. (1992), Introduction To The Constitution of India (Delhi: Prentice Hall Of India).

ChandraSekhar, S, (1988) Indian Federalism And Autonomy (Delhi: B.R. Publishing Corporation).

Paylee, M.C. (1977) Constitutional Government In India (Bombay: Asia Publishing House).

Ray, Bharati (1967) Evolution Of Federalism In India (Calcutta

:Progressive Publishers).

Dua. B.D., (1985) Federalism Of Patrimonialism: The Making And Unmaking Of Chief Ministers In India (Asian Survey)

Aiyar, S.P., And Usha, Mehta (1965) Essays On Indian Federalism (Bombay: Allied Publishers).

Kohli, Atul, (2009) Democracy And Development In India From Socialism To Post Business (New Delhi: Oxford University Press).

Chaube, S.K. (2000) Constituent Assembly: Springboard Of Revolution (New Delhi: Manohar)

Laski, Harold (2005) The Obsolescence of Federalism (New York: Palgrave Macmillan)

Rao, Shiva (1968) The Framing of India's Constitution: Selected Documents (New Delhi: Indian Institute of Public Administration).

Chabra, Harinder. K, (1977) State Politics In India: Study Of Centre-State Relations (Delhi: Surjeet Publication).

Banerjee, Anil Chandra (1977) The Constitutional History of India (Delhi: Macmillan Publishers)

Bhargava, P.K., (1982) Centre-State Resource Transfer in India (Gurgaon: Academic Press).

Dua, B.D. And Sing, M.P., (2003) Indian Federalism IN A New Millennium (New Delhi: Manohar).

Gadgil, D.R., (1947) The Federal Problem of India (Poona: Gokhale Institute of Politics And Economics).

Karat, Prakash (2004) Federalism and Political System in India (Delhi: Marxist).

Fadia, B. L., (2012) Indian Government and Politics (Agra: Sahitya Bhawan).

Patil, S.H. (2006) Changing Bases of Federal Units in India Vol. 1 & 2 (New Delhi: Mohit Publication).

Saxena, Rekha (2003), Role of Intergovernmental Agencies in Federal India (New Delhi: Manohar Publisher).

Ray, Amal, (1979) Federal Politics And Government (New Delhi: The Macmillan Company of India Limited).

Saez, Lawrence (2002) Federalism Without A Centre (New Delhi: Sage Publication).

Ram, Sundar (2007) Federal System And Coalition Government in India (Delhi: Kanishka Publisher).

Patil, S.H. (2006) Changing Bases of Federal Units in India Vol. 1 & 2 (New Delhi: Mohit Publication).

Ambedkar, B.R. (1939) Federation Vs. Freedom (Bombay: Shree Laxminaryan Press).

Bose T.C. (1987) Indian Federalism: Problems And Issues (Calcutta: K.P. Bagchi).

Bombwall, K.R. "The Finance Commission and Union State Relation in India", Indian Journal of Public Administration, April- June 1964.

Chaube, S.K. "Analysis of Social Basis of Federalism, "Indian Journal of Political Science, October-December, 1987.

Verney, D.V., "Resisting Federalism "Seminar, (357) May 1989.

Bahl, A.K., "Post War Development in Federalism", Indian Journal of Political Science, October-December 1960.

Rao, K.V., "Centre-State Relations in Theory and Practice," Indian Journal of Political Science," Vol. XIV, Nov, October-December 1953.

Singh L.S. and Nanda Kumar, U.K., " Restructuring Indian Federalism with Special Reference To Article 356", U.P. Journal of Political Science, 2 (2); July – December 1990.

Mishra, G . "Centre-State Relations and Polls" Link 27 (19) 16 December 1984.

Livingston, W.S., "A Note on the Nature of Federalism," Political Science Quarterly, Volume 67, 1952.

Dau, B.D., " Federalism or Patrimonialism: The Making And Unmaking of Chief Ministers In India", Asian Survey 25 (8) ; August 1985.

Gopalkrishnan, P.K., "Centre-State Relations in Finance and Planning" Mainstream, 22 (46) July 14, 1984.

Joshi, Ram and Desai, K.D., "Towards A More Competitive Party System in India," Asian Survey, November 1978.

Situating India on the World Map India's Rise Narrative and Rethinking Cohen's World Geopolitical Order

Deblina Mukherjee

Abstract

Since her independence in 1947, India has come a long way in the power hierarchy of the world state system. This image of India as a confident emerging power with cross-regional interests and superpower status prospects has developed recently. In his famous theorizing of geopolitical structure of the world, Saul Bernard Cohen accorded India an important country status but kept her confined to the 'geopolitical region' of South Asia in distinction from the 'geopolitical realms' and other major countries of the world having cross-regional interests and operational abilities. Nehru's India had a foreign policy vision that was worldwide in scope after independence but subsequent bilateral conflicts and continuously uneasy bilateral relations at the subcontinent level resulted in her inward vision and placed her in the 'policy trap' of South Asia or what Raja Mohan dubbed as continent focused 'Hindu tradition of Indian Statecraft'. A narrative about a country's position involves understanding that respective leaderships or segments of leaderships hold about their own country's global standings, interests and goals, the way they formulate policies that promote a particular image and the understanding it creates in others in given circumstances. Both material elements and subjective elements are important for conjuring up an image. The paper will focus on the geopolitical visions and worldviews, geopolitical code constructions and policy formulations by the strategic elite which gave India the new image from the 1990s onwards. The break from the geopolitical policy trap of South Asia , her forays eastwards, westwards and southwards, resultant change of status and the nature of relationships with several major and minor actors and birth of new regional discourses have created the possibility of change in Cohen's geopolitical world structure which this paper seeks to explore.

Keywords: India, Foreign Policy, Geopolitics, Cohen, Indo-Pacific.

> *"For in Asia and around the world, India is not simply emerging, India has already emerged..."*
>
> -Barrack Obama (2010)

> *".....This is a country which has amazed the world over the last few decades with its growth and its development, the world's second most populous country; on purchasing power terms, the world's third-largest economy, clearly, the emerging democratic superpower of the world"*
>
> -Tony Abbott (2014)

Both these viewpoints, the first by the President of the United States of America and the second by the Prime Minister of Australia, are a microcosm of the various perceptions that exist about India in the policy establishments of different countries. Multiple narratives on the 'rise' of India as a global power are available and scholarship on that is multiplying. Majority of these narratives end with a positive tone telling a story of India's rise thereby framing an overarching discourse whereby epithets of 'rising', 'emerging' are becoming commonplace when referring to India.

This image of India as a confident emerging power with cross-regional interests and superpower status prospects has developed in recent times. As Stephen P. Cohen (2001, 1) observes,

"To its smaller neighbours, India has always been a great power. It has had a strong impact on their cultures, their economies and even their identities. This power has been of great concern to Pakistan, the only state in the region to have challenged India. To China, most western states, Japan and the economic and political arrivistes of Southeast Asia, however, India has not counted among the most important states of the world."

India was seen as breaking free of this image primarily from the 1990s onwards giving rise to the new narrative as the discussions in the upcoming sections of the paper will portray.

The Idea of Geopolitical Visions, Discourses, Narratives and their Relation to Foreign Policy Formulations:

Ever since Halford Mackinder wrote his famous piece "*The Geographical Pivot of History*" in 1904, 'geopolitics' has turned out to be a very popular theoretical framework for 'understanding' and 'interpreting' international relations as well as one for analysing foreign policy. Most simply understood in the classical sense, geopolitics is the 'scholarly analysis of the geographical factors underlying international relations and guiding political interactions' (Cohen, 11). Originally coined by Swedish political scientist Rudolph Kjellen in 1899 and popularized by Mackinder, it fell into disrepute due to negative translation of German geopolitician Karl Haushofer's ideas by Hitler. After facing a temporary blow, the concept was revived by Henry Kissinger in the Cold War years as a domain of everyday practical power politics and ever since it has come back in academic deliberations in different guises. This was the school of classical geopolitics. Grounded in what is known as 'cartesian perspectivalism'(Tuathail 1996, 23) , this tradition had an objective approach. The world, in this case, is taken as a reality that exists outside the consciousness of the individual and hence possible to study in a neutral fashion. The organ of perception, in this case, is a 'monocular eye, a single eye removed from rest of the body' and the function of that eye is to 'witness' and not 'interpret' (Tuathail 1996, 24). This viewpoint came to be challenged by the school of critical geopolitics which brought the idea of Foucaltian discourse into the analysis of geography.

Critical geopolitics denied the objective existence of geopolitical knowledge as a neutral detached description of reality. It has a highly ideological and political connotation and hence linked geography to discourse. Very simply put, discourses are ways in which knowledge is produced through language and is represented. It is an important form of power. A narrative, on the other hand, is a storyline. It is a way in which particular events are presented as stories based on factual and imaginative elements and these stories then go on to frame the understanding of people about their outside world. Narratives are the constituent elements of a discourse. Geopolitics as a discourse is a culturally and politically varied way of describing, representing and writing about geography and international politics (Tuathail 1998, 3). It is a discursive practice by which intellectuals of statecraft (whole community of state bureaucrats, leaders, foreign policy experts and advisors) throughout the world specialize international politics in such a way as to represent it as a world characterized by particular types of peoples, places and dramas (Tuathail and Agnew 1998, 79-81)and act accordingly. As these frame our understandings of places and in turn, the policies attached to those places, foreign policy of a state hence can be said are products of such discursive practices. As Dijkink (1996, 1) notes, "to live within a territory arouses particular but shared visions (narratives) of the meaning of one's place in the world and global system." (Dijkink 1996, 2). Foreign policy of a state is also an exercise in the construction of the identity of a state.

Thus we can see that foreign policy has a very important geopolitical dimension. It involves the construction of meaning and adding value to places. When we discuss the foreign policy of a state, it is important to draw attention to the narrative functions of a state's 'privileged storytellers' (Dodds 1993, 71) like policy makers, academic experts, media, foreign policy professionals. These storytellers, the circumstances which framed those stories the resultant policies and their effect on the ongoing circumstances together frames the identity of the practicing country and generates policy reactions from others as well.

Now we can move to a discussion on the idea of geopolitical visions. Dijkink (1996,11) defines *geopolitical visions* as " any idea concerning the relation between one's own and other places, involving feelings of (in) security or (dis) advantage (and/or) invoking ideas about a collective mission or a foreign policy strategy." It requires the creation of a *national identity*, an 'us' and 'them' distinction and emotional attachment to that distinction. Another element of a vision is a *geopolitical code* which simply put is a list of friendly and hostile nations in a given point of time. It also involves the idea of a *national mission* which may reflect various aims and the last important element is the *foreign policy belief system* i.e the set of lenses through which decision makers perceives their environment and frame policies. (Dijkink 1996, 11-13) and by decision makers, it is meant the whole community of political leaders, state bureaucrats, foreign policy experts and advisors. The subsequent discussion in the paper will briefly highlight the changing geopolitical visions of India, the foreign policy outcomes of those visions and the resultant status India received in the foreign policy framework of other countries.

India and her Geopolitical Visions: Evolution of the Narrative of a Rising Power

India started her journey as an independent country with a foreign policy orientation that was global in reach. Nehruvian internationalism was intent on giving civilizational India a position that counts in world politics. On numerous occasions, he had stated his views about India's place in the world. In his speech to the Constituent Assembly, March 8, 1949 Nehru said (Nehru 1949, 21):

> "The Indian Union is an infant State, infant free State, a year and a half old, but remember that India is not an infant country. India is a very ancient country with millennia of history behind her – a history in which she has played a vital part not only within her own vast boundaries but in the world and in Asia in particular."

Based on the pillars of foreign policy autonomy in a cold war world, anti-colonialism and third world solidarity, Nehru gave the world India's first foreign policy orientation and geopolitical vision – nonalignment. He gave India a geopolitical code which upheld the spirit of friendship and nonviolent international relations. There was the narrative of a peace-loving India who had the ability to exercise influence without using coercion. India's nonalignment policy and the anti-West flavour because of links to anti-colonialism and anti-imperialism alienated her from the foreign policy calculations of countries like United States of America (USA) whose interests were pinned on countries who were becoming part of the bloc politics of Cold War. India also misread the formation of the pro-western ASEAN as a copy of SEATO and her closed economy was also, in turn, was not attractive to these countries in the region.

India followed a geopolitical code of regional 'brothers', a foreign policy belief system based on liberal internationalism and a national mission of a champion of peace even on the face of adversities and conflict mediator which fell flat in the harsh realities of the Cold War world. The defeat against China in 1962 totally shattered the global geopolitical code and shifted India's policy priorities. International ambitions got trapped in the immediate environment of regional threats.

As Dijkink (1996, 131) observed,

"Internal antagonisms, the sheer size of India's population and territory and the daily burden of material survival shape a sub-continental world whose internal problems absorb most of the political energy and interest that Indians can produce."

This trend continued in post-Nehru years but the foreign policy belief system displayed changes. As David Malone(2011, 47) observes:

"India's journey from 1947 till the present day, both in terms of foreign policy and domestic politics, can be seen as a transition from idealism under Nehru, through a period of 'hard realism' (or realpolitik) lasting roughly from the mid

1960s to the mid 1980s (coinciding with the dominance of the Indian political scene by Indira Gandhi) to economically driven pragmatism today."

1966 was the watershed year when Indian worldview changed with Indira Gandhi came into the political scene. Not only did she centralize politics at the domestic level but also attempted to assert Indian position at the regional level and dispel the notion of India as a passive state. The tilt towards Soviet Union, assistance in Bangladesh Liberation War splitting Pakistan into two halves, Pokhran nuclear tests of 1974, incorporation of Sikkim into the Indian Union in 1975 can be cited as landmark events. India's national mission in that period turned out to be about carving a role for herself that was commensurate to her size in the region. Her policies led to the formulation of the term Indira Doctrine similar to American Monroe Doctrine. This doctrine found its origin in Bhabani Sengupta's writing in 1983 the crux of which was that India will neither intervene in domestic affairs of any state in the region unless requested to do nor tolerate such intervention by outside power and if external assistance is required to meet an internal crisis, states should first look within the region for help (Chacko 2012, 141). The assertion of image in the region was important because unless the neighbourhood is managed, the geopolitical code cannot be expanded and power credibility cannot be marketed at the cross-regional and global level.

During the Rajiv Gandhi years of 1980s normalization of relations with the west was started with Gandhi visiting the United States and addressing the US Congress. He visited China and the Soviet Union. He toured the world extensively and addressed international forums to make India's voice heard and tried to boost her global image. He responded to calls of the neighbourhood assisting the Maldives in 1988. He tried to assist Sri Lanka in her ethnic crisis by sending the Indian Peacekeeping Force to mediate and bring but unfortunately failed costing him his own life. Gandhi was the first in line to try to bring in economic liberalization to India through light reform policies and emphasised on encouraging science and technology for a better India. The reform policy which he initiated reached its crescendo in 1991 when India entered the arena of globalization. However, the basic premises of foreign policy displayed continuity. It was the tactics that displayed change to some extent.

The end of the Cold War ushered in new challenges for India. A reassessment of roles became necessary. The balance of payments crisis forced India to open up her economy and become a part of the globalized world through her New Economic Policy. The huge market that India provided increased her attractiveness globally. Nuclear tests of 1998 added up to hard power quotient of India. At the regional level, cooperative spirit and soft power projection was brought in reflected in the Gujral Doctrine of 1996 which talked about non reciprocal unilateral assistance and accommodation of needs of smaller neighbours, no interference in internal affairs, peaceful settlement of disputes and respect for territorial integrity and sovereignty indicating continuity of Nehruvian vision politics. Break up of Soviet Union brought in the imperative to diversify external relations. Non – alignment had to be given a new meaning and multi-alignment seemed a viable alternative and thus began Indian extra-regional connectivity drives.

The biggest foreign policy shift in this decade was the Look East policy that for the first time dedicated India's attention to a rapidly growing 'extended neighbourhood' and also re-established India's age-old ties with the east. Subsequently, focus has been placed on looking west, north and south as well.

Before we go into a brief summary of these links we can briefly look at the new popularized foreign policy orientation of India which is being referred to as the rise of the Modi Doctrine (Ganguly, Chauthaiwale and Sinha 2016). Under Manmohan Singh administration Indian foreign policy had maintained a steady pace. The mission had been to increase India's economic strength displayed in the constant growth rates even when the entire world seemed to face a downturn and diversification of external relations. Since Narendra Modi became the Prime Minister in 2014, there have been constant efforts to boost the international image of India. A string of foreign visits bolstering commercial diplomacy, defence diplomacy, diaspora connect, cultural diplomacy with different regions of the world has become a part of Indian diplomacy promotion. Slogans like 'India First' and policies like Make in India, Digital India, Skill India or Smart Cities is a branding win for India setting aside questions of success or failure of such initiatives. The geopolitical vision of India is once again seen to develop a global dimension with geopolitical code construction attempts cross-regionally, a national mission to build a new reinvigorated India and a foreign policy belief system that is influenced by the discourse of India moving on the path of greatness.

The extra-regional links of India can be highlighted as follows:

Looking East

Immediately after independence Nehru had attempted to build up eastern solidarity, but it was given the formal launch by Prime Minister Narasimha Rao in his Singapore lecture, September 1994 and officially mentioned in the Ministry of External Affairs Report of 1995-96. He laid emphasis on building strong economic and security relationship between India and her eastern neighbours. Since then this policy has evolved in phases and dimensions. The initial focus of this policy was placed on primarily Association of Southeast Asian Nations (ASEAN) countries and on economic and institutional partnership but later on it expanded in what was referred to as Look East Phase- II in which the security dimension was added. Hailed as a success this policy stance has been maintained by all successive governments. In November 2014, speaking at the Annual Summit of the ASEAN, Indian Prime Minister Narendra Modi (2014) talked about the establishment of an "Act East" policy emphasizing on a more active engagement with ASEAN and other countries in her east. India's eastern engagement since the 1990s paid off in different directions. Certain instances can be provided-

> ➢ In North East Asia relations improved most prominently with Japan followed by South Korea. With both these

countries economic relations have improved significantly. With Japan the relation went steps ahead with December 2006 Joint Statement towards Japan-India Strategic and Global Partnership and similar such joint partnership declarations and the October 2008 Joint Security Declaration. In November 2016 India and Japan signed the Agreement for Cooperation in Peaceful Uses of Nuclear Energy. This is a very important sign of the nature of relationship because India is the only non NPT signatory country who received an exemption from Japan. Militarily India and Japan have common interests in securing the sea lanes in Asia Pacific and Indian Ocean and is seen carrying out bilateral and trilateral exercises like JIMEX and MALABAR.

➢ In Indo-China region the country with which India shares the most cordial relation is Vietnam. After the collapse of USSR and later on with the flaring up of South China Sea disputes, Vietnam has sought to diversify her foreign relations and relations has improved with India. 2003 saw the signing of a Joint Declaration of Comprehensive Cooperation Framework between India and Vietnam. Wide ranging defence cooperation has developed over time with a peak reaching in 2016 when a credit line has been given to Vietnam for defence equipment acquisition including possible BrahMos cruise missile. Joint oil exploration drives in the disputed South China Sea waters and grant of docking rights to Indian Navy in South Vietnam few kilometres away from the finest deepwater shelter in the region, Cam Ranh Bay are other developments.

➢ In maritime Southeast Asia the country closest to India in terms of cordiality is Singapore. Given its strategic location with respect to the straits of Malacca relations with this country is extremely crucial for India. Both economically and militarily relationship has prospered between these two countries. In 2005 Comprehensive Economic Cooperation Agreement has been signed. Since

1993 these two countries have been conducting joint military exercises like SIMBEX and MILAN and India has even granted access to Indian facilities for Singapore air force and army training.

➤ Relations have improved with Indonesia mainly economically but it also has security aspects like joint patrol agreements for ensuring the security of navigation at the entry points to Malacca Straits. With Australia security cooperation has been formalized in 2009 with a Joint Declaration on Security Cooperation. Australia is part of the joint Malabar naval exercise along with USA, India and Japan. 2014 saw the signing of India-Australia Civil Nuclear Cooperation Agreement.

➤ Priority is also being given to Pacific island nations like Fiji where very recently in 2014; USD 75 million of credit was extended by India along with an agreement to expand their defence and security cooperation (*The Indian Express* 2014).

However, it was not just the east that India focused her attention to. Policies were directed towards the west, north and south as well.

Looking West and Connecting North

The oil-rich West Asia is obviously an important region to guide India's diplomacy given the latter's energy needs and a huge diaspora in that region bringing in a huge amount of remittances to India but formal policy developments have been a recent affair. The energy needs clause apply to the Central Asian region as well. India has developed economic and security relations with a number of countries in the region. It has good relations with Iran, Saudi Arabia, Israel, Iraq, and the Gulf States. India has signed defence agreements with several countries in the region including Bahrain, Saudi Arabia, Qatar, Oman, United Arab Emirates (UAE). The process had geared up from Manmohan Singh administration and 2015 saw the official announcement of the Look West policy. The policy was unveiled by Narendra Modi in the Joint Statement that he signed with the UAE leadership on August 17, 2015. As Sanjay Baru (2015) notes, through his famous Singapore lecture, Narasimha Rao unveiled India's "Look East" Policy, through the Joint Statement that he signed with UAE's leadership, Mr. Modi has unveiled India's Look West policy. The agreement on Chabahar port facility development with Iran ((May 2016) and Modi's visit to Israel in 2017 are two landmarks in India's West Asian orientation.

India's connections with Central Asia also go back ages. Modern Central Asia comprises of Kazakhstan, Kyrgyzstan, Tajikistan, Turkmenistan, and Uzbekistan. This region now is an area where the game of control over energy resources is going on and India could not have been left out in the game. The Connect Central Asia Policy (CCAP) was given official status at First India- Central Asia Dialogue on June 12, 2012. The key elements of this policy cover many important issue areas, including political cooperation, economic cooperation, strategic cooperation, regional connectivity, information technology (IT), cooperation in education, people-to-people contact, medical cooperation, and cooperation in regional groupings (E Ahamed 2012). As border contact with the region is not there, India's venture to reach the region via Chabahar Port development agreement is a golden opportunity thereby bypassing Pakistan to connect Central Asia through West Asia.

Looking South: The Maritime Dimension

India is looking towards the sea for power projection, unlike earlier times. As the largest littoral state at the head of the Indian Ocean, India has always had a geographical advantage. India today is willing to exploit this advantage and has advocated an extension of area of interest of operation for India. The words of Minister of Defence, Manohar Parrikar (2016) are important as they point out this extended area of interest of India-

"For India, located as we are at the centre of the Asian landmass astride the Indian Ocean, any reference to Asia implies its fullest geography ranging from the Suez to the shores of the Pacific."

It is to be noted that immediately after independence, focus on economic development had resulted in the sidelining of defence planning in the country. The adversities faced in the Indo-China war brought about a change in perception but initial focus was on the armed forces. India began to assert her naval position in the region only from 1970s onwards on the eve of Bangladesh Liberation war and after that has incrementally increased her role to become a security provider in the region the process of which speeded up from the 1990s after India entered the globalization framework when the importance of oceans came to be realized both economically and strategically.

Not only the logistic capabilities are increasing but also the spheres of influence are increasing through commercial and security relations with littoral states in Indian and Pacific Oceans. Such relations exist and in other process with several countries like Singapore, Indonesia, Vietnam Maldives, Oman, Qatar, Iran, Mauritius, Seychelles, Mozambique, Madagascar and has also been a sponsor of forums like Indian Ocean Naval Symposium.

With China continuing expansion of operations to the Indian Ocean region, Indian Navy is also expanding their operation from Gulf of Aden to Straits of Malacca and even moving beyond that to the disputed South China Sea region as part of cooperative multi-nation military exercises which are also held in Bay of Bengal, Arabian Sea, Gulf of Aden and Cape of Good Hope areas. India's naval modernization is gearing up and the role of the navy is expanding. Surface fleet, naval aviation, submarines and acquisition of other state of the art technology are all on the rise. India now has maritime doctrines, maritime strategies, blue water fleet, tri-lateral command and a cross regional operational interest.

India and multilateral frameworks

When India gained independence, global multilateral framework comprised mainly of United Nations (UN) and allied organizations. She became a founding member of the organization and had great faith in the framework until disillusioned by the treatment of the issue of Kashmir by the organization. During the 1950s India followed a policy of active neutrality playing positive roles in the Korean crisis and first phase of the Vietnam crisis keeping up the image of a champion of world peace. The post world war decolonization process which led to the emergence of a number of newly independent countries provided India with an opportunity to be a champion of 'third world' interests in multilateral frameworks like GATT negotiations, expansion of Security Council, formation of G77 group within the UN, formation of United Nations Conference on Trade and Development (UNCTAD) to name a few. The Cold War intensification kept the United Nations divided and hence less effective until the 1990s. From the 90s decade onwards India actively became part of peacekeeping missions and in important negotiations on issues like environment. As India's role kept on increasing, there was a need felt in the foreign policy circles of the country for a recognition of the same. Thereafter India started the demand for permanent membership to the UN Security Council along with countries like Brazil, Germany and Japan.

Dr. Manmohan Singh (2005) clearly stated the following in his speech to the Joint Meeting of the US Congress as the Indian Prime Minister,

"Globalization has woven a web of interconnections all around the world. This makes it all the more necessary that we evolve a system of global governance that carries credibility and commands legitimacy. Such a system must be sufficiently participatory.... there must be comprehensive reform of the United Nations to make it both more effective and more representative. The United Nations Security Council must be restructured as part of this reform process... in this context ...*the voice of the world's largest democracy surely cannot be left unheard on the Security Council when the United Nations is being restructured...*" (Italics for emphasis)

Currently, India has been able to garner support for her permanent candidature to the UN. On April 16, 2017 Sushma

Swaraj, External Affairs Minister was heard stating that India had all the credentials to become a permanent member of the UN Security Council and four permanent members, the US, the UK, France and Russia, had extended support to its bid (*The Times of India* 2017) indicating a welcome change in India's image. Apart from UN, India has also diversified her multilateral framework engagement over time like G-20, SAARC, ASEAN, Shanghai Cooperation Organization, IBSA (India, Brazil, South Africa) and BRICS. She has also become part of Missile Technology Control Regime and is garnering support for becoming a part of the Nuclear Suppliers Group.

Apart from the above orientations, relations with USA is also taking a positive turn. Normalization attempt started during the tenure of Rajiv Gandhi has been followed up by all subsequent establishments. As the discourse of China rise looms alarmingly in the US imaginations driving them to look for prospective partners to balance that rise, a rising India seems to be an effective solution to them.

The entire purpose of the aforesaid discussion has been to establish the fact that Indian geopolitical visions, codes, national missions and foreign policy belief system have undergone changes over time. From a global code to a regional and back to global, India has come a long way since independence.

The narratives of the rise of India seem to have found its believers in a large number of countries encompassing the littoral areas of the Indian and Pacific oceans. The looking up to India as a prospective partner and foreign policy overtures of India towards such expectations is seen giving rise to a new regional construct which is being referred to as 'Indo-Pacific' or Indo-Asia Pacific in several quarters.

Indo-Pacific: India's Rise and the New Regional Narrative

The world map is replete with regional labels. Certain labels have become so much popular over time with repeated usage that they have acquired a common-sense status but still disputes prop up now and then regarding geographical limits and sometimes even with names of regions. This shows that describing and delimiting a region on the world map is a contested idea. To quote the words of E.W Gilbert (1960, 158),

"the art of describing a region- and I do consider it to be an art, for it is futile to regard it as an exact science with universal laws- is quite as difficult as the art of describing the character of a human individual... regions, like individuals, have very different characters; moreover, the characters of regions, like those of individuals, are constantly changing or developing."

Borrowing the analytical lens of critical geopolitics, it can be stated that a position on a map is not just a mere physical location that can be understood by material realities alone but rather the art of imagination employed behind it has to be uncovered too to complete that understanding. Regional labels are imagined ones stamped on particular regions by actors whose interests seem to be benefited by them. Regions are social constructions linked to aspirations, hopes and fears of actors and reflect power relations as well which in turn are narratives created by storytellers in policy and academic establishments based on interpretations of reality in the light of the discourses they believe in. The rise of the Indo-Pacific is the present discourse that has captured the imagination of many policy establishments and is fed by multiple narratives like the rise of China, decline of USA, need for balancing and containing China and rise of India to name the few prominent ones.

This new construct as it has developed is considered to be an extension of a earlier popular construct- Asia Pacific and is a 21st century phenomenon. The construct of Asia Pacific had excluded India from consideration but given Indian policy shifts and actions the "the mental map of Asia Pacific has changed and the centre of gravity has moved westward to include India." (Rao, 2013)

The term Indo-Pacific found its origins in an article by Indian analyst Gurpreet Khurana (2007) in the context of Indo-Japan cooperation in securing sea lanes of communication. The official usage of the term Indo-Pacific first came from the Japanese Prime Minister Shinzo Abe in 2007 and since then it had made reappearances in statements and official documents of Japan, Australia, Indonesia and even in references by USA.

Australian Defence Minister Stephen Smith (2011) in a speech to the Asia Society, Mumbai stated,

"In this century, Asia, the Indian Ocean region and the Pacific will become the world's centre of gravity. Everyone sees the rise of China, but not enough see the *rise of India as a great power*. The *rise of India* remains under appreciated, as does its standing as the world's largest democracy. *India today is assuming the mantle of global influence to which its economic size and strength, and its strategic weight and history entitle it*... Australia welcomes this because we see in *India a country that has a constructive role to play* in our region and *on the world stage...so significant is India's rise that the notion of the Indo-Pacific as a substantial strategic concept is starting to gain traction...*"(Italics for emphasis)

The policy establishment of Australia has gone a step further with a *Defence White Paper*(2013) becoming the first country to formally name its area of engagement as Indo–Pacific and has appeared in their defence white papers of later years as well.. The paper states,

"A new Indo-Pacific strategic arc is beginning to emerge, connecting the Indian and Pacific Oceans through Southeast Asia. This new strategic construct...is being forged by a range of factors. Notably, *India is emerging as an important strategic, diplomatic and economic actor, 'Looking East', and becoming more engaged in regional frameworks*. Growing trade, investment and energy flows across this broader region are strengthening economic and security interdependencies. ... The Indo-Pacific is still emerging as a system. Given its diversity and broad sweep, its security architecture is, unsurprisingly, a series of sub-regions and arrangements rather than a unitary hole...the influence of (other) regional powers such as Japan, the Republic of Korea, and Indonesia, is becoming more important. Although the strategic environment will be shaped largely by the relationship between the United States and China, and by the *rise of India* in the longer-term, the increasing number of influential Asian states means we are witnessing the evolution of a more complex and competitive order."

The Indo Pacific voice is also being heard from the United States of America on several occasions. Hillary Clinton during her 2011 India visit spoke about India's importance to the Asia Pacific region. In her words (Clinton 2011),

> "Today, the stretch of sea from the Indian Ocean through to the Pacific contains the world's most vibrant trade and energy routes linking economies and driving growth. The United States has always been a Pacific power because of our very great blessing of geography. *And India straddling the waters from the Indian to the Pacific Ocean is, with us, a steward of these waterways.* We are both deeply invested in shaping the future of the region that they connect and that India should not just look east but 'engage East." (Italics for emphasis)

The usage of Indo–pacific terminology is slowly becoming common in the Indian foreign policy establishment as well as in the academia. Indo-Pacific has reappeared on several occasions from different commentators and from various forums. Shyam Saran's written piece in *The Indian Express* titled *Mapping the Indo-Pacific* (Saran, 2011) played a very important role in popularizing the construct. In his words,

> 'Over the past year, the term "Indo-Pacific" has gained currency in strategic discourse in India... It is a logical corollary to India's Look East policy having graduated to an Engage East policy. The fastest growing component of India's external economic relations is its engagement with ASEAN, China and Japan and, more lately, Australia. This has resulted in a growing density of maritime traffic through the Indian Ocean and radiating all along the Western Pacific

littoral. These have created a seamless stretch of ocean space linking the Indian and Pacific Oceans...*As India's regional and global profile increases, it will inevitably gravitate towards the centre of this expanded geopolitical and geo-economic space. The concept of an Indo-Pacific theatre fits in neatly with this evolving trend...*' (Italics for emphasis)

After having a glimpse at the narratives which are being woven, we can move to the position accorded to India by the most extensive theorizing of the geopolitical structure of the world.

Saul Bernard Cohen's World Geopolitical Structure and Status of India:

In his popular work *Geopolitics: The Geography of International Relations*, Saul Bernard Cohen (2009) extensively theorized about the geopolitical world structure based on political developments across the world. He talked about three hierarchical spatial levels operating in two major geographical settings which are either maritime or continental:

- ➢ The *geostrategic realm* which comprises parts of world large enough to possess characteristics and functions which are globally influencing and serve the needs of major powers, states and regions they comprise.

- ➢ The *geopolitical regions* which are subdivisions of realm forming the middle level

- ➢ *National states, autonomous regions, quasi-states* and *territorial subdivisions* within and across states at the lowest level forming the micro level. (Cohen, 2009; 33,37)

The following table will provide the basic structure at a glance:

Table 1

Major Geopolitical Realm	Geopolitical Regions	Major/First Order Country
Atlantic and Pacific Trade Dependent Maritime Realm	North and Middle America, South America, Maritime Europe and Maghreb and Asia Pacific rim	United States of America
Eurasian Continental Realm	Heartland Russia, former Soviet Republics of Eastern Europe, trans-Caucasus and Central Asia	Russia
Mixed Continental Maritime East Asia	Mainland China, North Korea and Indo- China embracing Vietnam , Laos Cambodia	Peoples Republic of China

Source: Saul Bernard Cohen, Geopolitics: The Geography of International Relations, 2009, Rowman and Littlefield Publications Inc, USA

South Asia as a region and India as a country is not seen featuring in any of the realms. Cohen kept it separate as an independent geopolitical region. The countries he included in this region are India, Pakistan, Bangladesh, Sri Lanka and Maldives, Nepal and Bhutan while referring to Myanmar as a bordering country connecting this region to East Asia and Asia Pacific Rim. (Cohen, p.329) The dominance of India in the region, however, has been kept intact with the speculation that *in the long term this region may evolve "into a realm that embraces the Indian Ocean Basin"* (Cohen,42)

Now, this seems to be on the path of realization as a culmination of India's looking, acting, engaging east and far east as well as acting south. Based on the popularity of India's rise narrative and the new regional construct, the question that can be raised here is whether it will alter the geopolitical structure of the world. Hence as a follow up to aforesaid prediction we can attempt to add a fourth realm named the *Indo-Pacific Maritime Realm* to Cohen's world geopolitical structure as given in Table 1 earlier. This realm if framed will turn out to be inter-regional. It will take in parts of South Asia (India), parts of mainland Southeast Asia (Myanmar, Vietnam), North East Asia and Asia Pacific Rim countries (Japan, South Korea, Singapore Indonesia, Australia and Pacific Islands like Fiji). This new probable realm can also be treated as an ally realm of the first given the involvement of the United States in the former. As the region under question is huge and there exists a host of powers with economic and strategic capabilities, identifying a single major country is difficult at this juncture. Rather than a single country, a loose coalition can be identified that is leading element in this probable realm. Triggered by the need to secure the commons and the sea lanes of communication and 'geopolitical anxieties' and 'imaginations' of China's rise (Pan 2014, 455-456) cemented by China's assertiveness in the region along with development of strategic and military capabilities of India , development of a new pragmatic strategic culture and normalization of relations with a host of countries over time underpinned by the narrative of *rise of India,* this new regional discourse has taken shape. She is no longer trapped at the subcontinent level as was thought when creating the original structure. It is true that the 'Indo' in the 'Indo-Pacific' is not India but the Indian Ocean but given her location, her capabilities and the code of friendly countries she has developed for herself over time there cannot be a 'Indo-Pacific' without India and irrespective of criticisms the 'rise' cannot be ignored.

Conclusion

Jawaharlal Nehru had a vision reflected in these words (Nehru [1946] 1989, 536),

> "The Pacific is likely to take the place of Atlantic in the future as the nerve centre of the world. Though not directly

a Pacific state, India will inevitably exercise an important influence there. India will also develop as the centre of economic and political activity in the Indian Ocean area, in Southeast Asia and right up to the Middle East. Her position gives an economic and strategic importance in a part of the world, which is going to develop rapidly in future."

These words written before independence, display an instance of the kind of geopolitical vision the first Prime Minister had, a vision that India would rise to be a power that would have cross-regional imprints. Over time, many deficiencies have been dealt with and new strengths have been discovered. Both in terms of hard power and soft power abilities, India has improved. Both a believer and a nonbeliever of the narratives of India's rise have to admit the improvements that India has made in 'absolute' terms though lagging behind in 'relative' terms. All these improvements are reflected in the huge audience that India's rise narrative has throughout the world both academically and politically and the way in which it is shaping and will shape the national foreign policy of other countries and regional discourses in the days to come.

References

Abbott Tony. (2014, September 9). Remarks at the Prime Minister's Business Delegation Breakfast, Mumbai, India. Transcript. http://pmtranscripts.pmc.gov.au/release/transcript-23792.

Ahamed.E. (2012, June 12). "India's 'Connect Central Asia' Policy". Keynote Address. First India-Central Asia Dialogue. Bishkek. Kyrgyzstan. http://www.mea.gov.in/ Speeches Statements.htm? dtl/19791/Keynote+address+by+MOS+Shri+E+Ahamed+at+First+I ndiaCentral+Asia+Dialogue

Baru, Sanjay. (2015, August 19). "The Sprouting of the 'Look West' policy". *The Hindu*, http://www.thehindu.com/opinion/lead/sanjaya-baru-writes-the-sprouting-of-the-look-west-policy/article7554403.ece

Chacko, Priya. (2012). *India's Foreign Policy: The Politics of Post*

Colonial Identity from 1947 to 2004, London: Routledge

Clinton, Hillary. Rodham. (2011, July 20), "Remarks on India and the United States: A Vision for the 21st Century".Speech. Anna Centenary Library. Chennai, India. http://www.state.gov/ secretary/20092013clinton/ rm/2011/07/168840.htm

Cohen, Stephen.P. (2001). *India: Emerging Power*. New Delhi: Oxford University Press

Defence White Paper.(2013). Department of Defence. Government of Australia. http://www.defence.gov.au/ whitepaper/2013/docs/ wp_2013_web.pdf

Dijkink, Gertjan.(1996). *National Identity and Geopolitical Visions: Maps of Pride and Pain*. London. New York: Routledge

Dodds, Klaus.J. (March, 1993). Geopolitics, Experts and the Making of Foreign Policy. *Area*. 25(1), 70-74. http://www.jstor.org/ stable/20003214

Ganguly, Anirban., Vijay Chauthaiwale and U.K.Sinha. (Eds. 2016). *The Modi Doctrine: New Paradigms in India's Foreign Policy"*. New Delhi: Wisdom Tree India

Gilbert, E.W.(July,1960). The Idea of the Region: Herbertson Memorial Lecture. *Geography*.45 (3), 157-175. http://www.jstor.org/ stable/40565156

Indo-Asian News Service. (2012, November 14). "Clinton lauds India's role in Indo-Pacific region, urges for increased participation". *India Today*. http://indiatoday.intoday.in/story/hillary-clinton-lauds-indias-role-indo-pacific-region-talks-china-breifly-in-australia/1/229136. html

Khurana, Gurpreet S, (2007). Security of Sea Lines: Prospects of India-Japan Coooeration , *Strategic Analysis*, 31(1), 139-153. doi:10.1080/09700160701355485

Malone, David. (2011). *Does the Elephant Dance: Contemporary Indian Foreign Policy*. New York: Oxford University Press

Modi, Narendra. (2014, November 12). Remarks by the Prime Minister at 12th India-ASEAN Summit. Nay Pyi Taw. Myanmar. http://www.mea.gov.in/Speeches-Statements.htm? dtl/24236/ Remarks+by+the+Prime+ Minister+at+12th+IndiaASEAN+Summi t+Nay+Pyi+Taw+Myanmar

Natalegawa, Marty. (2013, May 16). "An Indonesian perspective on the Indo-Pacific". Speech. Centre for Strategic and International Studies Conference on Indonesia .Washington DC. https://csis-prod. s3.amazonaws.com/s3fs.../130516_MartyNatalegawa_Speech.pdf

Nehru, Jawaharlal. (1949). India's Place in the World. In. B.R. Nanda (Ed.). *India's Foreign Policy: Select Speeches September 1946-April 1961*. (1961). New Delhi: The Publications Division. Ministry of Information and Broadcasting. Government of India

Nehru ,Jawaharlal. (1989). *The Discovery of India* .Calcutta: The Signet Press; Centenary edition by Oxford University Press

Obama, Barrack. (2010, November 8). "Remarks by the President to the Joint Session of the Indian Parliament in New Delhi. India".Speech. https://obamawhitehouse.archives.gov/the-press-office/2010/11/08/ remarks-president-joint-session-indian-parliament-new-delhi-india

Pan, Chengxin. (2014). The 'Indo- Pacific' and geopolitical anxieties about China's rise in the Asian regional order, *Australian Journal of International Affairs*, 68 (4), 453-469. http://dx.doi.org/10.1080/103 57718.2014.884054

Parrikar, Manohar. (2016, June). Speech of the Defence Minister Shri Manohar Parrikar. Speech. Shangri-La Dialogue. Singapore. http:// pib.nic.in/newsite/PrintRelease.aspx?relid=145975.

Press Trust of India.(2014, November 19). "PM Modi seeks stronger ties with Fiji: announces a 75 million dollar credit line". *The Indian Express.* http://indianexpress.com/article/india/india-others/india-extends-75-million-dollar-credit-line-to-fiji/

Rao, Nirupama. (2013, February 4). "America's "Asian Pivot: The View from India". Lecture. Brown University,Australia.http://brown. edu/initiative/india/sites/brown.edu.initiatives.india/files/uploads/ NirupamaRao-America's'AsianPivot'TheViewfromIndiaInitiativeSe minar2.4.2013.pdf

Saran, Shyam. (2011, October 29)."Mapping the Indo-Pacific". *The Indian Express*http://archive.indianexpress.com/news/mapping-the-indopacific/867004/

Singh,Manmohan.(2005,July 19). Prime Minister Dr. Manmohan Singh's Address to Joint Session of the Congress. Speech. Washington. DC.

http://www.mea.gov.in/Speeches-Statements.htm?dtl/ 2613/Prime_
Minister_Dr_Manmohan_Singhs_Address_to_Joint_Session_of_
the_Congress

Smith, Stephen. (2011, December 9). "Australia and India Building the
Strategic Partnership".Speech. Asia Society. Mumbai.http://www.
minister.defence.gov.au/2011/12/10/minister-for-defence-australia-
and-india-building-the-strategic-partnership/

The Times of India. (2017, April 7). India deserves to become a
permanent member of the UN Security Council: Sushma Swaraj.
New Delhi.http://timesofindia.indiatimes.com/india/india-deserves-
to-become-a-permanent-member-of-un-security-council-sushma-
swaraj/articleshow/58057000.cms

Tuathail Gearoid .O.and John Agnew. (1992) Geopolitics and Discourse:
Practical Geopolitical Reasoning in American Foreign Policy .In. O
Tuathail, Simon Dalby and Paul Routledge (Eds.) *The Geopolitics
Reader* (E-Library version 2003,79-81). Retrieved from http://www.
tandfebooks.com/doi/view/10.4324/9780203444931

Tuathail, Geaoroid.O. (1996). *Critical Geopolitics: The Politics of
Writing Global Space.* London: Routledge

Tuathail, Gearoid.O. (1998). Thinking Critically about Geopolitics. In.
Gearoid O Tuathail, Simon Dalby and Paul Routledge (Eds.), *The
Geopolitics Reader* (E-Library version 2003,1-12). Retrieved from
http://www.tandfebooks.com/doi/view/10.4324/9780203444931

Maoist Movement and Its Effect on Indian Political System

Puspitarani Bardhan

A Maoist Party i.e. the Communist Party of India-(Maoist) which derives its ideological and militaristic inspiration from China's Mao Tse Tung's thought which propagates agrarian armed revolution to capture political power. CPI-(Maoist) spread one-third of the geographical area of the country through its mass organisation. The Party was formed by merging of various communist groups such as CPI-(ML), Peoples War Group, Maoist Communist Centre (MCC), CPI-ML Party Unity. The CPI (Maoist) aims to consolidate its power in the area like Bihar, Chhattisgarh, West Bengal, Maharashtra, Odisha, and Jharkhand and establish a compact revolutionary zone from which to advance the people's war in other parts of India. The Indian Government claimed that in 2013, that there is the ideological influence of "Left Wing Extremism" in Andhra Pradesh, Arunachal Pradesh, Assam, Bihar, Chhattisgarh, Delhi, Gujarat, Haryana, Kerala, Madhya Pradesh, Odisha, Punjab, Tamil Nadu, Tripura, Uttarakhand, Uttar Pradesh and West Bengal. Maoism and Maoism is a social and economic problem but more so it is now an internal security threat. In early 70s counted blocks and villages were the centre of Maoist and Maoistite Movement but in current scenario, each state is facing this problem as well. The problem of Maoism is because of the failure of the policy and plan meant for the development of the people of the country. The Maoist cadre took advantage of dissatisfaction of the people and started attracting them to their own group to solve their problem in the village itself. It is believed that in 2006

India's intelligence agency, the Research and Analysis Wing estimated that 20,000 armed- cadre Maoistites were operating in addition to 50,000 regular cadre and their growing influence prompted Indian Prime Minister Dr. Manmohan Singh to be the most serious internal threat to India's national security. Maoistites, Maoist and other anti-government militants are often referred to as "ultras". The present government led by Sri Narendra Modi, he also believed that the Maoist and Maoist problem needs to be solved in the interest of the development of the people of India.

Origin

The term Maoistites comes from Maoistbari, a small village in West Bengal, where a section of the Communist Party of India (Marxist) (CPI-M) led by Kanu Sanyal and Charu Mazumdar initiated a violent uprising in 1967. The strategy was the elimination of the feudal system in the Indian country side to free the poor peasants from the clutches of the oppressive landlords and replace the old system with a communist society that would implement land reforms. The Maoistite movement came down drastically in early 1970's due to state actions and death of Charu Mazumdar. Apart from the state repression, several splits within the Maoistite movement in the 1970s had weakened its capacity to resist the police and army offensive. Many followers had opposed the tactics of the assassination of individual 'class enemies'. As a result, the Communist party of India, Marxist Leninist (CPI M-L) was split into several factions with growing instances of infighting. The movement resurfaced in 1980 in Andhra Pradesh under the leadership of K. Seetharamaiah with a new organisation named, CPI (ML) - People's War Group. Although the movement started with the old demand 'land to the tiller', later, tribal rights, forest issues and industrialisation dominate with the pass of forest bills in 1980's and economic reforms in July 1991 respectively. Over the years, there is a qualitative change in Maoist Strategy from "land to the tiller" to "anti- globalisation" propaganda. The 1980s witnessed the peak of the Maoist movement when different segments of the society such as students, workers, peasants, women and to some extent the middle class, had become effective tools of revolution. People from these segments become the ideologues who could inspire the imagination of a movement. By 1990s, inflow into the Maoist movement from these two vital segments almost dried up due to employment opportunities in private sectors as India adopts the liberal economic policies. It is against this condition the CPI-Maoist has undertaken an exercise to redefine its response to the emerging situation. There is also visible change in the Maoist strategy and target groups. They have been targeting security forces, government officials, multinational corporations, landlords, railways establishments and other institutions in the name of their class struggle. Since 2000 onwards the Maoists are engaged in a strategy of seeking support from forcible displaced local tribal groups and minority groups in India. The cadre recruitment among these tribal groups to the Maoistites outfit has been increasing upwardly, so also the sympathy from the common people. The Maoists also do not abruptly launch into armed struggle or violence but are known for gradual consolidation, including a preliminary study of local social, economic and political conditions and the vulnerabilities of particular populations to the Maoistite mobilisation. However, the CPI-Maoist and other LWE outfits are also carrying out struggle changes in their movement by creating the support structures in big cities and urban areas in a strategic attempt to adapt to the changed socio-economic and security scenario.

CPI-(Maoist) Ideology and Methods

Mao-Tse-Tung's Ideology

The life and work of Mao assumes a great deal of importance as far as the present study is concerned. Mao's success lies with the fact that he not only combined Marxism-Leninism, but also made a comprehensive study of Chinese society and formulated appropriate tactics for Chinese revolution. Mao put the peasantry at the forefront of his revolutionary formula and made 'land reforms' as the central issue on which the capture of state power was premised. Mao laid great emphasis on guerrilla warfare and maintained that the revolution would proceed as a national war of liberation, which would begin along in the countryside and culminate in the capture of cities. It is on the basis of his understanding of the Chinese society and evils of imperialism; he designed the course of Chinese Revolution with the concept of armed struggle, protracted war, guerrilla warfare and self-reliance. Mao, makes sure not to miss a point when he writes in the context of Chinese revolution that, "it is wrong to belittle armed struggle, the revolutionary war, guerrilla war and army work." He moves on to write that, "Without armed struggle, neither the proletariat, nor the people, nor the Communist Party would have any standing at all in China and it would be impossible for the revolution to triumph. In these years [the eighteen years since the founding of the Party] the development, consolidation and bolshevization of our Party have proceeded in the midst of revolutionary wars; without armed struggle the Communist Party would assuredly not be what it is today. Comrades throughout the Party must never forget this experience for which we have paid in blood." For him the 'just goal' i.e. the establishment of people's government was important and with this in mind he formulated all his strategies and tactics, which could help him, win the war. In his own words, "our war is sacred and just, it is progressive and its aim is peace. The aim is peace not just in one country but throughout the world, not just temporary, but perpetual peace." To him armed struggle was a means to attend humanly life, which was under the clutches of imperialism. Throughout he maintained that war was not an act of adventurism but a necessity. "We are advocates of the abolition of war, we do not want war, but war can only be abolished through war, and in order to get rid of the gun it is necessary to take up the gun." Mao never preached mindless application of violence and hence was no anarchist. He was more concerned about revolution and for this, he laid great emphasis on armed struggle. To put it straight forward he wrote, "A revolution is not a dinner party, or writing an essay, or painting a picture, or doing embroidery: it cannot be so refined, so leisurely and gentle, so temperate, kind, courteous, restrained and magnanimous. A revolution is an insurrection, an act of violence by which one class overthrows another."

CPI-(Maoist) Party Ideology

The CPI-(Maoist) accepts Marxism-Leninism-Maoism as its guiding ideology and is committed to completing a new democratic revolution in India. The party carried out and completed through an armed agrarian revolutionary war, i.e. protracted people's war with the armed struggle for the seizure of power as its central and principal task. The party work against the imperialism, feudalism and comparator bureaucratic capitalism. The party also supports the struggle of the nationalities for self-determination, including the right to secession and the fight against social oppression, particularly untouchability and casteism and give special attention to mobilizing and organizing women as the mighty force of revolution. The party has added Maoism to be a part of their guiding ideology. They have heavily borrowed the strategy and aims of the revolution from that of Chinese revolution completed 56 years ago and no serious lessons have been drawn from the great set back to the international communist movement, the collapse of socialism, the big changes in the national and international situation and the specificity of the Indian political system and economy. The CPI(Maoist) documents are keener to highlight the violent nature of its revolution than the revolutionary aims. The party propose is to seize power through armed struggle. The Communist Party of India (Maoist) claim that they are conducting a "people's war", a strategic approach developed by Mao Zedong during the guerrilla warfare phase of the Communist Party of China. Their objective is to install a "people's government" via a New Democratic Revolution. The party also views Islamist militancy as a struggle towards national liberation against imperialism, rather than as a clash of civilizations, and condones it as having parallel goals to the group's own. In the words of deputy leader Koteshwar Rao, or Kishanji: "The Islamic upsurge should not be opposed, as it is basically anti-US and anti-imperialist in nature. The Communist Party of India (Maoist) is the consolidated political vanguard of the Indian proletariat. Marxism-Leninism-Maoism is the ideological basis guiding its thinking in all the spheres of its activities. Immediate aim or program of the Communist Party is to carry on and complete the new democratic revolution in India as a part of the world proletarian revolution by overthrowing the semi-colonial, semi-feudal system under neo-colonial form of indirect rule, exploitation and control and the three targets of our revolution—imperialism, feudalism and comprador big bourgeoisie. The ultimate aim or maximum programme of the party is the establishment of communist society. This New Democratic Revolution will be carried out and completed through armed agrarian revolutionary war. During the whole process of this revolution the party, army and the united front will play the role of three magic weapons. In their interrelationship, the party will play the primary role, where as the army and the united front will be two important weapons in the hands of the party. Because the armed struggle will remain the highest and main form of struggle and army as the highest form of organization of this revolution, hence armed struggle will play a decisive role.

History of Maoist Movement

The Communist Party of India (Maoist) is an ultra-leftist political party in India which aims to overthrow the government of India through people's war. It was founded on 21 September 2004, through the merger of the (People's War Group), and the Maoist Communist Centre of India (MCCI). The Communist Party of India (Maoist) claim that they are conducting a "people's war", a strategic approach developed by Mao Zedong during the guerrilla warfare phase of the Communist Party of China. Their eventual objective is to install a "people's government" via a New Democratic Revolution.

A Left-wing or leftist is a member of Communist guerrilla groups in India, mainly associated with the Communist Party of India (Maoist). Maoistites, and other anti-government militants, are often referred to as "ultras". The term *Maoist* derives from the village name Maoistbari in West Bengal. Maoistites are considered far-left radical communists, supportive of Maoist political sentiment and ideology. Their origin can be traced in 1967 of the Communist Party of India (Marxist) led by Charu Mazumdar and Kanu Sanyal initiated a violent uprising in 1967. The centre of this movement is in West Bengal. In later, it spreads developed areas of rural southern and eastern India, such as Chhatisgarh, Odisha and Andhra Pradesh. In 2006 India's intelligence agency, the Research and Analysis Wing estimated that 20,000 armed-cadre Maoistites were operating in addition to 50,000 regular cadres and their growing influence prompted them to be the most serious internal threat to India's national security.

The left-wing extremist (LWE) movement in India can be divided into four phases. Those are (i) Maoistite phase (1967-1972), (ii) Dormant or Splinter group phase(1972-1980), (iii) Dominance of People's War Group and Maoist Communist Center of India phase (1980-2000) and (iv) United Front against state repression (2000 onwards...). In the Maoistite phase, the Maoistites fought against the land owners and demanded for the land. The strategy was the elimination of the feudal system in the Indian country side to free the poor peasants from the clutches of the oppressive landlords and replace the old system with a communist society that would implement land reforms. The Maoistite movement came down drastically in early 1970's due to state actions and death of Charu Mazumdar. Apart from the state repression, several splits within the Maoistite movement in the 1970s had weakened its capacity to resist the police and army offensive. Many followers had opposed the tactics of the assassination of individual 'class enemies'. As a result the Communist party of India, Marxist Leninist (CPI M-L) was split into several factions with growing instances of infighting. The movement resurfaced in 1980 in Andhra Pradesh under the leadership of K. Seetharamaiah with a new organisation named, CPI (ML)- People's War Group. Although the movement started with the old demand 'land to the tiller', later, tribal rights, forest issues and industrialisation dominate with the pass of forest bills in 1980's and economic reforms in July 1991 respectively. Over the years, there is qualitative change in Maoist Strategy from "land to the tiller" to "anti- globalisation" propaganda. The 1980s witnessed the peak of the Maoistite movement when different segments of the society such as students, workers, peasants, women and to some extent the middle class, had become effective tools of revolution. People from these segments become the ideologues who could inspire the imagination of a movement. By 1990s, inflow into the Maoistite movement from these two vital segments almost dried up due to employment opportunities in private sectors as India adopts the liberal economic policies. It is against this condition the CPI-Maoist has undertaken an exercise to redefine its response to the emerging situation. There is also visible change in the Maoist strategy and target groups. They have been targeting security forces, government officials, multinational corporations, landlords, railways establishments and other institutions in the name of their class struggle. Since 2000 onwards the Maoists are engaged in a strategy of seeking support from forcible displaced local tribal groups and minority groups in India. The cadre recruitment among these tribal groups to the Maoistites outfit has been increasing upwardly, so also the sympathy from the common people. The Maoists also do not abruptly launch into armed struggle or violence but are known for gradual consolidation, including a preliminary study of local social, economic and political conditions and the vulnerabilities of particular populations to the Maoistite mobilisation. However, the CPI-Maoist and other LWE outfits are also carrying out struggle changes in their movement by creating the support structures in big cities and urban areas in a strategic attempt to adapt to the changed socio-economic and security scenario.

Maoist Movement in different Regions

According to current estimates Maoist movement active in 156 districts of 13 States that include Andhra Pradesh, Chhattisgarh, Jharkhand, Bihar, Orissa, Uttar Pradesh, Madhya Pradesh, Maharashtra, West Bengal, Karnataka, Tamil Nadu, Uttaranchal and Kerala. It expands its presence in several other States such as Gujarat, Haryana, Punjab, Rajasthan and Himachal Pradesh. The MCC's current areas of influence extend over Bihar and Jharkhand, with some sway in Uttar Pradesh, Chhattisgarh, Orissa, West Bengal, Uttaranchal and a few pockets of Madhya Pradesh. The PWG's areas of dominance include Andhra Pradesh, Orissa, Chhattisgarh, Karnataka, Maharashtra and Tamil Nadu.

Maoist Movement and its effect on political system of India

The CPI (Maoist) continues to be the most potent among the various LWE outfits in the country and accounted for more than 80% of total LWE violent incidents and resultant deaths. Amidst increasing reverses, the CPI (Maoist) made efforts at reviving erstwhile strongholds along inter-State boundaries with the intention to divert the attention of the SF from its core areas. However, revival efforts by Maoists in Jharkhand, Andhra Pradesh-Odisha border areas, establishment of a base at the tri-junction of Kerala-Karnataka-Tamil Nadu and formation of a new Zone at the tri-junction of Madhya Pradesh-Maharashtra-Chhattisgarh did not meet the desired success due to periodic interdictions of senior leaders by the SF. While extortion/ levy activities by the Maoists continued, the demonetization drive by the Government of India delivered a major dent to their finances. The Maoists tried to strengthen coordination between its mass organizations and other like-minded organizations to undertake programmes against alleged state violence and for protection of democratic rights. The government of India taking major steps to deal with the movement and now the movement is not so much active in nature but its working is going on through the political party i.e the Communist Party of India-Maoist. The government of India wakening and try to deal with the problem of Maoism so that, in February 2009, the Indian Central government announced a new nationwide initiative, to be called the "Integrated Action Plan" (IAP) for broad, co-ordinated operations aimed at dealing with the Maoist problem in all affected states namely Karnataka, Chhattisgarh, Odisha, Andhra Pradesh, Maharashtra, Jharkhand, Bihar, Uttar Pradesh, and West Bengal. Importantly, this plan included funding for grass-roots economic development projects in affected areas, as well as increased special police funding for better containment and reduction of maoist influence in these areas. In March 2012 Maoist rebels kidnapped two Italians in the eastern Indian state of Odisha, the first time Westerners were abducted there.

The government has constituted an 'Empowered Group of Ministers' to counter the problem of Maoism headed by the

Home Minister and select chief minister. The government under the Unlawful Activities Prevention Act (UAPA), 1967 amended in 2004 has banned the Communist Party of India (Marxist-Leninist) - People's War and all its associated formations, and the Maoist Communist Centre (MCC) and its front organizations. The government has also constituted a Task force which will comprise of Nodal officers from the Maoist affected areas and officers from the IB, SSB and the CRPF. There is also a Coordination Centre that was set up in 1998 headed by the Union home minister with Chief Secretaries and DGPs of the Maoist affected areas for the coordination of steps taken to control Maoist activities. The government has laid down a clear plan to tackle the left wing extremism. It has formulated a two-pronged strategy to solve the problem of Maoism/Maoism.

The tribal and scheduled castes that live in the Maoist affected areas have been neglected for the past many decades and now want some attention from the government. Providing them with incentives like giving them right over the forest produce from the forests in which they have been living for generations, providing them with houses etc. is the right modus of solving their basic problems. The main reason for the spread of Maoism is the exploitation of poor and scheduled castes. The main thing which has to be done is to enforce land ceiling laws, utilization of the funds provided to the government to the maximum and political expediency. Use of police forces should be to enforce the land ceiling laws, evict landlords and ensure land to the farmers for cultivation. They should be provided with police protection, and proper rehabilitation for the people who have been displaced should be ensured. The government has constituted an 'Empowered Group of Ministers' to counter the problem of Maoism headed by the Home Minister and select chief ministers. The government under the Unlawful Activities Prevention Act (UAPA), 1967 amended in 2004 has banned the Communist Party of India (Marxist-Leninist) - People's War and all its associated formations, and the Maoist Communist Centre (MCC) and its front organizations. The government has also constituted a Task force which will comprise of Nodal officers from the Maoist affected areas and officers from the IB, SSB and the CRPF. There is also a Coordination Centre that was set up in 1998 headed by the Union home minister with Chief Secretaries and DGPs of the Maoist affected areas for the coordination of steps taken to control Maoist activities. The government has laid down a clear plan to tackle the left wing extremism. It has formulated a two-pronged strategy to solve the problem of Maoism.

The government has launched a Police Modernization Scheme in areas affected by Maoist movements. Under this scheme huge sums of money have been provided to the state governments by the central government to modernize their equipment and tactical gear including latest communication, vehicles and infrastructure facility. States have also been told to determine police stations and outposts that are susceptible to Maoist attacks and have to be fortified. Central Para Military Forces have been deployed on a long-term basis by the government to help the state governments to fight against the Maoist. The states have also been relieved from paying the charges involved in deploying these forces for about 3 years which nearly is about Rs.1100 crores. The government, also to discourage the youth from the path to militancy, has revised the recruiting guidelines to permit 40% recruitment in Central Para Military Forces from areas affected by Maoism. The government has also raised a special force of 14,000 personnel consisting of Central Paramilitary Forces, state police and ex-servicemen from areas affected by Maoism. Plans have been set in motion for the formation of three to four specialized Anti-Maoist Centres at critically important locations at inter-state boundaries which will be equipped with five helicopters each and would be manned by the CRPF and the pilots would be called from the Army/BSF/Air Force. The use of UAV's for reconnaissance missions and collection of intelligence from Maoist affected areas has been authorized by the Centre. The government of Chhattisgarh started the Counter Terrorism and Jungle Warfare College in Kanker imparts training to counter the well trained and motivated guerrilla force of the Maoists, where police personnel are given rigorous training in guerrilla warfare and are made to live in the open and taught how to live off the land. Even the Army who as such are not very interested in getting themselves dragged into tackling Maoism have been training 16 companies of paramilitary and state personnel in counter Maoism operations. States have also established their own special security force like Andhra Pradesh has formed the Greyhounds which are said to be one of the most effective police force to combat the Maoist problem and the government of Uttar Pradesh has also raised a battalion of the Provisional Armed Constabulary consisting of the local youth. Even the Central government has formed the COBRA which is a special force formed to deal with Maoism in any state.

The government of Karnataka also allocated special funds for development in villages affected by Maoist activities. Grama panchayats were provided with Rs. 10 lakhs a year for two years to develop the villages within their jurisdiction. Other grants from the government, zilla and taluk panchayats were also included to be used in the development of these villages. The government also requested the planning commission to include other Maoist affected areas under the Scheme of Backward Regions Grant Funds for which Rs.5000 crores have been set apart.

The government of Chhattisgarh has also announced houses worth Rs.1 lakh and employment to the kin of who got killed in the Maoist violence and the Jharkhand government increased the insurance amount to be given to the kin of jawans to 21.5 lakhs 45 from the 10 lakhs. Various schemes launched have been launched by the government like the Pradhan Mantri Gram Sadak Yojana (PMGSY) which offers tremendous opportunities for rural road connectivity. For certain districts affected by Maoism which have a population of 500 and above in plain areas and 250 and above in tribal areas 3 years perspective plans are being formulated to cover all habitations. The National Rural Employment Guarantee Programme (NREGP) is being implemented in 330 districts affected by Maoism so as to universalize the demand-driven programme for wage-employment. Other schemes which are in addition to the above-mentioned schemes are Bharat Nirman, National Rural Health Mission (NRHM), Sarva Shiksha Abhiyan (SSA), Integrated Child Development Services (ICDS) and other income generating and social security schemes of the Ministry of Rural Development, Agriculture, Panchayati Raj and Tribal affairs. The central government will also provide 100 percent assistance in the formation of Ashram schools and hostels for girls and boys in tribal areas. States like Jharkhand and Orissa have offered huge incentives to the Maoist who surrender themselves. Further, the government has offered cash equivalent to the price of the weapon surrendered. They will provide them with life insurance cover, vocational training, agricultural land, health and educational facilities for their children.

In 2016, the issue of displacement of local communities remained the main plank of mobilization by the mass organisations. In Niyamgiri Hills area (Districts Rayagada and Kalahandi, Odisha), the outfit continued to guide the activities of the Niyamgiri Suraksha Samiti. Similarly, in Jharkhand, the Visthapan Virodhi Jan Vikas Andolan a front of the CPI (Maoist), tried to take up pro-tribal issues and opposed amendments to the Chhotanagpur and Santhal Pargana Tenancy Acts, modifications in Domicile Policy etc. Maoist affiliates also undertook protest programmes and resorted to anti-Government propaganda over alleged atrocities by Security Forces. They organized similar meetings over the issue of Kashmir and called for a plebiscite in the State. With the Maoists forced to remain in a state of strategic defensive in most of the States, it is time to consolidate the gains in order to end this menace once and for all.

Conclusion

Maoism is a political issue and needs a long-term political solution. There is a complete lack of political involvement at the delivery level of these programs. The Indian government needs to ensure development and security policies are realised simultaneously to have a sustained impact in the Maoist regions. Social and economic rehabilitation programs to bring the discontented Maoists into the mainstream would be helpful. The state has to do much more than plan counter-insurgency operations or support violent vigilante groups to suppress the Maoist movement. After close examination of the historical and ideological origins of the movement, it is clear that the movement thrives on the dissatisfaction of the marginalized and alienates the population. The socio-economic perspective of Maoism talks about how the rebel movement is shaped due to the failure of the institutional mechanisms and frameworks to deliver socio-economic justice. This article outlines the steps taken by the government, but concedes that it is not enough to over-emphasize the 'law and order' approach. The people if not get their justice and always suppressed then the Maoist movement is going on. So there is need of a solution and the people and also the government will come forward and take initiatives to tackle the problems. There is need for development and proper implementation of programs and policies which are enforced by the government for the upliftment of the poor and downtrodden. It is clear that there is a wide gap between promises and their eventual deliverance. Until the government implements employment, poverty alleviation and land reform programmes, counterinsurgency measures cannot achieve much. Social justice and inclusive growth are the planks on which the government must build its programme. Only with consolidated efforts on the part of the legal and political framework socio-economic reforms can be implemented, and the problem of Maoism tackled.

The people if not get their justice and always suppressed then the Maoist movement is going on. So there is need of a solution and the people and also the government will come forward and take initiatives to tackle the problems. There is need for development and proper implementation of programs and policies which are enforced by the government for the upliftment of the underdeveloped people.

References

"India Maoists kidnap Italian tourists in Orissa". *BBC News.* 18 March 2012.

"Mortality and Burden of Disease Estimates for WHO Member States in 2002" (xls). *World Health Organization.* 2004.

"Annual Report 2010-2011," *Ministry of Home Affairs Republic Of India,* "2010 bloodiest year for India's Maoist rebellion," *AFP,* January 5, 2011.

Agarwal, Vineet, *"Romance of a Maoistite"* , New Delhi: National paperbacks, 2006.

Ahmed, Nadeem; 2003: Charu Majumdar – The Father of Maoism; in: Hindustan

Annual Report 2010-2011." Ministry of Home Affairs, Republic Of India.

Arundhati Roy, account of her travels with the Maoists in Bastar, *Outlook (*29 March 2010).

Banerjee, Sumanta, *"India's simmering Revolution"*, New Delhi: Select Book Syndicate, 1984.

Banerjee, Sumanta, *"In the wake of Maoistbari: A history of the Maoistites movement in India",* Subarnarekha, Calcutta,1980.

Banerjee, Sumanta, "Maoistbari: Between past and present", Economic and Political Weekly, June 01, 2002.

Bose, Prasenjit, *"Maoism: A critique from the left"*, edited book, published in may 2010.

Chakravarty, Sudeep, *"Red Sun: Travels in Maoistite country".* New Delhi: Penguin, 2008.

Dasgupta, Biplab, " *TheMaoistite Movement"* Allied Publishers, Calcutta,1974.

Drachkovitch, Milord M, *"Marxism in the modern world"* - Edited

Fanon, Frantz, *"The Wretched Of The Earth".* Translated by C.Farington. Harmondsworth: Penguin,1982.

Ghosh, Sankar, *"The Maoistite Movement: A Maoist Experiment",*

FirmalK.L.Mukhopadhyay, Calcutta, 1974.

Gupta, Dipak K, *"The Maoistites and the Maoist Movement in India: Birth, Demise, and Reincarnation,"* Democracy and Security, Vol. 3, (2007), pp. 157-188.

Gurr, Ted R., *"Why Men Rebel",* Princeton: Princeton university press,1970.

Ibid, p.3184.

Ibid, p.3185.

Jawaid, Sohail, *"The Maoistite Movement in India: origin and failure of Maoist revolutionary strategy in West Bengal".* New Delhi: Associate publishing house, 1979.

Jha, Sanjay Kumar, *Left Wing Terror: The MCC in Bihar and Jharkhand,* South Asia Intelligence Review, (www.satp.org), Vol. 1, No.40, April 2003.

Johari, J.C., *"Maoistite Politics In India",* Institute of Constitutional and Parliamentary Studies/ Research publications, Delhi, 1972.

K. Balagopal, 'Maoist Movement in Andhra Pradesh', *Economic and Political Weekly,* Vol.XLI, no.29 (22 July 2006), pp.3183-87.

Kamboj, Anil, Maoism: India's Biggest Security Challenge, Article No. 1995, Institute of Peace and Conflict Studies, (www.ipcs.org), 20 April 2006.

Karat, Prakash, *"Maoism Today; At an Ideological Deadend".*

Kujur, Rajatkumar "Maoism in India", human touch, vol .2 (6) ,june 2005.

Kujur, Rajatkumar And Charkabarty, Bidyut, " *Maoism in India; Reincarnation of ultra-left wing extremism in the twenty –first century".*

Kujur, Rajatkumar ,"Underdevelopment and Maoist movement". Economic and political weekly, vol.xli (7), 18-24 February 2006.

Kujur, Rajatkumar, *"Left extremism in India :Maoist movement in Chhattisgarh and Orissa".* .

Kujur, Rajat Kumar, *Andhra Pradesh and Maoist Outfits: Again on Collision Course,* Article no. 48, Society For the Study of Peace and

Conflict (ww.sspconline.org), August 25, 2005.

Kujur, RajatKumar, *"political violence: A theoretical discourse"*.

Kujur, Rajat Kumar. „Maoism in India". *Human Touch*, vol. 2 (6), June 2005.

Kujur,Rajatkumar, " *political violence: A theoretical discourse"*. Sambalpur University, journal of politics, vol.1.issue.1, March 2011.

Mohanty, Manoranjan, *"Revolutionary Violence: A Study of Maoist Movement in India,"* New Delhi Sterling publishers,1977.

Nayak, Giridhari, *"Neo-Maoistchallenge: issues and options".*

Nayak, Nihar, *"Maoist Movement in Urban India: Emerging Issues and Threats"*, Sambalpur University, journal of politics, vol.1.issue . 1, March 2011.

Websites:-

www.sspconline.org

www.ipcs.org.

www.satp.org

www.orfonline.org

National Security: Role of Energy in Terms of Oil and Natural Gas: Future Prospects With Reference to India

Rajneesh Kumar

What is the meaning of National Security?

Simply speaking, the National Security symbolizes a sense of confidence that the government of a sovereign state is able to instill into its citizenry through its proactive approach and actions. It is a comprehensive discipline encompassing not only the hard power but also the soft power in the form of various other politico-diplomatic and technological factors inherently related to a nation's entity as an independent politico-economic power enjoying global and regional diplomatic edge besides resultantly having the capability to realise its desired national interests by practicing strong diplomacy.

Therefore, in general, the idea of National Security broadly refers to various measures that a sovereign national government may adopt in course of fulfilling its cherished national objectives. Some of these measures include:

➢ Diplomatic actions to garner support of allies and isolate the proclaimed national enemy;

➢ Achieving economic prosperity;

➢ Attaining technological self-reliance;

➢ Modernization of its armed forces to pose a potent military deterrence;

- ➢ Achieving and sustaining the status of a nuclear power;

- ➢ Creating and sustaining a capability to tackle organized terrorist outfits through a strong counter intelligence network in close coordination with friendly nations;

- ➢ Creating and sustaining an effective infrastructure to tackle natural disasters;

- ➢ Capability to harness the international support for global issues like international terrorism, environment protection and climate change etc.;

- ➢ Achieving energy security for realising the objectives of infrastructure development;

- ➢ Projecting itself as a strong domestic political entity exhibiting influence as a strong national government;

- ➢ Creating and sustaining an effective infrastructure to tackle Cybersecurity; and

- ➢ Achieving and sustaining women empowerment.

Why does a government need to achieve and sustain National security?

The basic and foremost requirement for any national government is to have an effective infrastructure to achieve and sustain its national development objectives. This is also a key to ensure that the national government continues to enjoy a constant support of its populace and at the same time is also capable of refuting the opposition parties within the nation while at the same time inspiring and helping the other smaller countries in the region in their development process. This would help the national government not only in emerging as a strong national sovereign power within the national boundaries but also as a regional power internationally.

Changed connotations of National Security in modern times

However, the experience tells us that in today's market forces driven scenario, the economic and technological supremacy has come to surpass the significance of the hard-military power in helping a nation to emerge as a strong global power. Quoting the examples of China and Japan would be relevant in this regard. The USA despite having been known as a strong military power the world over since long, sustains an economy that is not self-sustaining. The US economy is rather dependent upon many other nations and factors for its sustenance. The USA is more often than not seen as constantly making all-out efforts for creating the support bases in South Asia mainly to safeguard its oil interests in the South Asian and Central Asian region. As a matter of fact, the US hegemony is seen declining owing to its demonstrated failures in tackling the war like situation in Afghanistan wherein it took years for the USA to nail down Bin Laden. This delayed success of US in neutralising Osama landed it in a situation wherein a major part of the world population started having serious doubts about thitherto proclaimed US might & nationalism and a popular belief in US traditional resolve of neutralising any and every force that challenged its hegemony or so to say its "freedom".

On the other hand, with the world assuming a multipolar posture in the recent years, the nations like China and Japan have emerged as technologically strong nuclear & space powers with their products inundating the international market in an unprecedented manner over the recent past. To top it up China has been able to build up its military capabilities also to a great extent thereby posing a potent threat to the political equilibrium in South Asia. Current Chinese advances in the North-Eastern part of India in collusion with Pakistan are posing real threat to the national security for India.

Is Infrastructural development cardinal to National Security and Why & how does Energy factor into the gamut of development?

Going by the recent trends in the international political scenario, there seems no doubt that the requirement of overall development plays a dominant role in any politico-diplomatic order of the day. The need for overall development, therefore, outweighs any and every consideration and challenges any belief that considers national security in the context only of security from enemies within and outside the national boundaries.

A very pertinent question that arises in this context is as to why is energy an important factor in the development crusade undertaken by any sovereign nation and how can this be harnessed to support the developmental aspirations of a nation. We all understand pretty well that the exercise of infrastructure development in never complete until the various parameters and indicators of development i.e. electricity, fuel and various other resources that are scarce, are available in abundance in any nation and that nation is able to have an uninterrupted supply thereof without any hindrances posed by any outside power.

Energy Security points to the presence of an institutionalised mechanism at the disposal of a sovereign national government to ensure an uninterrupted national accessibility to the diverse spectrum of precious energy resources and to achieve the availability of these in the right measure, at the right place, in the right time, at the right terms and most importantly, at the right price. The energy resources refer to the legitimate possessions at the hands of a nationality that are utilised for empowering it for undertaking and sustaining various developmental activities and activating the development infrastructure and various projects related thereto within its national and geographical boundaries.

These Energy Resources represent a wide array of national and international assets ranging from natural &physical to human resources that help in initiating and sustaining the process of infrastructural and economic development in a nation. The most relevant and crucial question that arises in this context impels a nation to think as to which type of resources are required to be tapped for a particular activity of development. It is undeniable that energy is essential for the economic growth and development of the country and hence has come to be recognised as a strategic commodity. Any uncertainty in the energy supply can threaten the functioning of any economy and therefore it becomes an imperative for any nation to secure energy supplies at affordable rates.[1]

What has been the Indian Experience?

The studies carried out so far with regard to India's energy security focus on addressing mainly the supply related issues through diplomatic and foreign policy instruments and domestic initiatives dealing with market distortions which deserve an equal attention.[2] To amplify the point in the context of international relations, energy is considered to be one of the most fundamental elements of the cosmos which has come to assume the properties of a 'strategic commodity' in the present century. Achieving energy security in the strategic sense is therefore of immense importance not only for developing countries like India for its multidimensional growth but also for the overall human development objectives of socio-economic and infrastructural growth which mainly aim at alleviation of poverty and eradication of unemployment which are considered as inevitable rudiments for meeting the Sustainable Development Goals (SDGs) in the 21st century which according to David Griggs and colleagues in the article "Sustainable Development Goals for Planet and People" published on UN.org mainly include protection of earth's life support systems to ensure smooth functioning of atmosphere, ocean, forests, waterways, biodiversity and biochemical cycles besides reduction of poverty.[3]Energy is essential for the economic growth and development of the country and hence has come to be recognised as a strategic commodity.[4]The lack of energy makes it a contentious issue among the competing nations and also has potential to lead to inter-state crisis thereby becoming an inter-state clash and ultimately assuming the contours of a potent international security hazard. The dearth of energy gives birth to inter and intra-state conflicts. Therefore, shortage of energy is regarded as one of the potent sub-conventional national security threats arising out of militancy and terrorism.

Presently, India stands at number five internationally considering its energy demands. However, despite this the Indian energy consumption is to the tune of mere 400 MMTOE against the world average of 1780 MMTOE. As per the Annual Report of Ministry of Petroleum & Natural Gas, Govt of India[5] for 2015-16,37.47 % of primary domestic energy consumption 28.33% of which comes from crude oil and 7.14% from Natural Gas. The report also brings out that during 2015-16 the average domestic gas production was around 86.59 Million Metric Standard Cubic Meter Per Day (MMSCMD) in India. This apart, the communiqué informs that as per the report of the working group on Petroleum & Natural Gas sector for 12th Five-year plan, the total demand of all the sectors of Indian economy (i.e. power, fertilizer, city gas, industrial, iron & steel and petrochemicals/refinery/internal consumption etc) was around 446 MMSCMD for 2015-16 (till Sept 2016) which is projected to be 473 MMSCMD for 2016-17, 494 MMSCMD 2017-18 and 523 MMSCMD for 2018-19[6]. As stated by Rajiv Sikri – a career diplomat[7], the overall energy mix of India is characterised by 51% of coal, 36% of oil, 10% of Natural Gas, 2% of hydropower and just 1% of Nuclear energy. India's share of hydro power may increase if India attempts at tapping the hydro power resources of neighbouring countries e.g. Nepal, Bhutan and Myanmar.

The improved rail-road network is the primary pre-requisite of infrastructure development which is also the KRA of the present-day government. Considering this, the pressure on the government for bringing about infrastructure development is expected to witness an upscale trend due to Development being the mandate of the popularly elected government. With this, the requirement for oil is expected to rise mainly for rail and road transportation sector while that of Gas is likely to rise for generation of electricity.

The undisputed overriding importance of energy security in the overall context of National Security is cemented by the fact, that in face of the constantly rising demands for energy in the years to come, the global oil and gas production are expected to be on decline. This is thus likely to create a world-wide gap between increasing demands and declining production[8].

In respect of India it was soon realised that in view of the national energy reservoirs depleting fast, the key to better energy management lies in the achievement of self-reliance in the arena of energy resources. A prudent way of meeting the shortfall of energy in India that was conceived was to reap the advantages of abundant energy resources located in the five republics of Central Asia i.e. Kazakhstan, Turkmenistan, Uzbekistan, Tajikistan and Kyrgyzstan.

India's historical connect with Central Asia

The historical evidence suggests that India had connectivity with Central Asia through trade and commerce which had roots also in the emotions emanating from successive invasions into Indian subcontinent mostly from the north-westerly directions during the past many centuries. Historically Central Asia had been culturally, emotionally and commercially important since ancient times. In modern times various powers mainly USA, China and Russia focused their attention on Central Asian Republics (CARs) in order to realise their economic interests which has brought in the strategic ramifications into fray.[9] Post-independence Indian ties with Central Asian states witnessed a change and came to be characterised by India's customary proximity to erstwhile USSR after the 1962 Indo-China war. However, notwithstanding this, India's footprint in the Central Asian region was sadly limited to mere cultural interactions. Thereafter the downfall of Soviet Union impelled a calculated swing in Indian foreign policy during 1990s necessitating a deliberate move towards more sensible politics-economic ties. Post change in the foreign policy focus, India started focusing towards mutually advantageous interactions with the five newly formed Central Asian republics.

On a realistic plain, India's energy demands witnessed a constant upscale trend truly proportionate with the manifest national power shortages caused by inadequate energy infrastructure in the country. A need was therefore felt to achieve greater energy diversification besides global cooperation with Central Asia. The Indian experience makes it clear that it is not feasible to find long-lasting solutions to the issues of energy security without resolution of security and political issues.[10] Apart from this, energy defines economic relations even within the society and it has power connotations too. Such linkage of energy to the national needs has come to make it an important determinant of foreign policy also because the trans-border and trans-national potential of energy trading heavily impinges upon the foreign policy in subtle as well as overt ways.[11] Indian leadership saw this as a preferred diplomatic option which was influenced by the availability of abundant oil, gas, and uranium reserves and hydroelectric richness considering it as catalyst for plummeting India's energy dependency on the turmoil infested West Asian states.

The recent discovery of fresh resources did not instill sufficient confidence in the nation due to security and foreign policy related concerns. This drove home an urgent need to involve Public-Private-Partnership (PPP) model into the exercise of harnessing the energy resources. Therefore a need was felt to match the opportunities prevailing in the global energy industry and the world's economic surpluses among oil exporters with the specific needs of India.[12]

Recent International developments with respect to Energy Security

The present government immediately after settling down in late 2014 realised the indisputable need for energy security more than the other factors inherent into the spectrum of National Security. The realization was guided more by the resolve of the government for a technologically advanced e-India wherein all the governmental as well as the non-governmental agencies had a paramount role to play.

The Indian Foreign Policy astutely focused its attention on tapping of the energy resources located in Central Asia in a deliberate and consensual manner backed by an aggressive diplomatic approach. The lightening visits of the Indian Prime Minister to various world powers within a short span of time resulted into smooth diplomatic relations beginning to be formed with many of the world powers. The government started treading the path of mutual give and take which inspired and encouraged many countries like USA, Russia and to a great extent Japan also to agree to a definite conviviality as far as the goal of harnessing the energy resources of Central Asia goes.

The US lifted the sanctions imposed since long on Iran opening gates to a major trade activity. Iran had been at a strategic position in the entire gamut of harnessing the energy resources located in Central Asia. The move was guided by the US desire to maneuver Iran into the main stream of oil trade in the region. In respect of India, the Indian leadership had clearly understood that any passage of energy resources from Central Asia has no other convenient route but through Iran and Afghanistan. While China was focusing since long on the uplift of Gwadar Port, India started thinking in terms of reaping the advantages of Chabahar Port.

How Chabahar Port could be useful and What are the likely takeaways in the form of Energy Security for India?

The Indian Prime Minister visited Iran on 23-24 May 2016 and opened floodgates to India's willingness to invest initially $ 20 Billion in Iran's petrochemical, fertilizers and Liquefied Natural Gas (LNG) facilities and in turn seeking cheap natural gas and land to set up the units. This was followed by an agreement to invest about $ 500 Million for development of the Chabahar Port located 120 Km West of China's own Gwadar Port in Pakistan's Balochistan province. The Times of India[13] writes that *Chabahar will rid India of its dependence on Pakistan for access to Afghanistan and energy-rich Central Asia where Beijing's influence continues to grow by leaps and bounds*. Maj Gen (Dr) GD Bakhshi[14] also has opined that the development and opening of Chabahar Port would enable transportation of oil and natural gas from the Central Asian energy reservoirs into Indian territory via Arabian Sea completely bypassing the Pakistani territory.

Indian Ports Global would create 640 meters berthing facilities 2 container berths and 3 multi-cargo berths as part of this deal. India will also spend close to $ 1.6 Billion and task The IRCON to build a railway line from Chabahar to Zehadan which would link up with Zaranj-Delaram Road connecting it with Afghan road network. This apart the deal also aims at creating Iron mines, Aluminium Smelter Plants besides Urea making units in Chabahar Free Trade Zone area.

As a matter of fact, the security of the oil pipeline traversing Pakistan has since long been giving goosebumps to India due to its security being perpetually on the tenterhooks, thanks to the traditionally strained relations between India and Pakistan. But with Chabahar Port becoming operational, this trust deficit which was rendering the transportation of energy resources from Central Asia would be totally negated. The new route to be followed now would be from Turkmenistan in Central Asia–Afghanistan Delaram–Zaranj–Zahedan–Iranshah–Chabahar Port crossing the Arabian Sea and landing at Kandla port or Mumbai port into India. The ease of transportation and creation of logistics facilities in Chabahar Free Trade Zone by India would lead to a mutual win-win situation not only for India but also for Iran and Afghanistan besides Central Asian Republics from where the oil and gas reserves would be obtained.

This apart, as the operations of transporting the energy resources resume, the Indian public sector especially India Ports Global, Indian Railway Construction Co. Ltd (IRCON) and ONGC Videsh are likely to be fully immersed into realization of the Indian dream of *Sabka saath sabka vikas* with employment generation for the Indian youth. Though the exact quantum of employment generation is yet to be worked out by the government, the investment proposed to be made by India is aimed at future energy security as well as the creation of a robust energy infrastructure besides generating long-term dividends in terms of employment and enhancement of national income. Economic Times dated 23 May 2016 also writes that India stands to gain a lot from Chabahar deal inked by the Indian Prime Minister. In short, the major takeaways for India are:

> India will develop and operate the Chabahar port. India Ports Global, will invest $85 million in developing two container berths with a length of 640 meters and three multi-cargo berths. The contract is for 10 years and extendable. It will take 18 months to complete phase one of the port construction. The first two years of the contract are grace period which means India doesn't have to guarantee any cargo for the port. From the third year, India will facilitate 30,000 TEUs (Twenty Foot Equivalent) of cargo at the port. The quantum will rise to 2,50,000 TEUs by the 10th year.

> State-run railway body IRCON International will set up a railway line at Chabahar to move goods right up to Afghanistan. The 500-km rail link between Chabahar and Zahedan will link Delhi to the rest of Iran's railway network.

> Also, as part of the agreement, a free trade zone is to be created where a total investment of INR 1 lakh crore is envisaged. Indian companies would set up a range of industries from aluminium smelter to urea plants in the region. State-owned NALCO will set up an aluminium smelter while private and co-operative fertiliser firms are keen to build urea plants.

> India will also supply $400 million of steel rails to Tehran. There are plans of a fertilizer plant through a joint venture with the Iran government. Securing hydrocarbon sources is a priority for India as Delhi and Tehran would look to expand the basket in the coming years.

What prompted India to go for this move and what are the future prospects for India?

Perhaps besides the aim of attaining ease of transporting the energy resources into India, the main guiding factor was that no other international port has as strategically been located as Chabahar for India considering the need to reduce dependence on trouble-torn West for transportation of energy resources ex-Central Asia. As it stands, the operationalization of this port will definitely enable India to bypass Pakistan in transporting goods to Afghanistan using a sea-land route.

This apart, it is also expected to activate the International North-South Transport Corridor and Iran happens to be the key gainer in this project. It would necessitate the creation and operationalization of ship, rail, and road routes for moving freight between India, Russia, Iran, Europe and Central Asia. The route primarily involves moving freight from India, Iran, Azerbaijan and Russia. The corridor would increase trade connectivity between major cities such as Mumbai, Moscow and Tehran.

Over and above anything and everything, it is definitely expected to counter Pakistan assisted Chinese presence in the Arabian seaby developing Gwadar port. Chabahar Port can be used strategically and tactically by India to deploya Naval fleet for the security of the merchant ships off the African coast besides providing India a strong foothold in the western Arabian Sea.

More importantly, in furtherance of the Trilateral pact signed between India-Iran-Afghanistan in May 2016, recently Japan too has expressed willingness to help in the development of Chabahar Port to facilitate Afghanistan's access to the Chabahar Port. The Times of India[15] writes that a multi-cornered cooperation on connectivity will provide Afghanistan an assured and alternative access to regional markets contributing to the development, peace and stability in the country.

What effect will the energy security have on Indian rationale of National Security?

As stated, the availability of a stable and reliable infrastructure is a must for the realising the dream of overall national development or nation-building. The experience tells us that it's not only India but any other third world or developing country would intelligently and rationally focus its eyes on the idea of development of infrastructure and facilities more than the development of military power. In today's world, the overall wellbeing is the hallmark of development. The population having secured means of livelihood in terms of secured employment and having a capability & willingness to contribute to the process of nation-building are the order of the day found in any country irrespective of whatever faith or type of political system it may follow.

The energy is an incontestable resource which is the driving force in the national development process. We have understood that the abundance of energy would positively help in the process of development, and also that its dearth would hamper the process thereof. On a serious note, the shortage of energy backed by a competitiveness on part of the national governments of the developing nations competing with each other in striving for the energy security have a potential to push these nations into strife with each other. This might also lead to a situation wherein one competing nation becomes an adversary and attempts at destabilizing its opponent in every possible way.

The availability of energy, therefore, is an irrefutable influence in the concept of national security and any prudent &intelligent government would follow it up as a major KRA to live up to the expectations and confidence which the people of the nation repose in it in the form of the popular mandate. The governments of the day largely come to power on the agenda of development whether it be the Parliamentary or the presidential form of government. Therefore, the agenda of development, by virtue of directly impinging upon the national security puts energy security at the forefront of any nationalistic activity which a popularly elected government embarks upon to meet the requirements of national security especially when creation and sustenance of energy security outfits also meets the requirements of technological and economic development of the country.

The present Indian government realised it and strategically started thinking in the direction of achieving the energy security as part of national security through vigorous diplomatic efforts. The Indian government is moving positively fast on the track of killing many birds with one stone in this regard.

In short, the successful multipronged strategy of the present government aims at attaining a wide spectrum of long-term objectives:

> Securing the energy resources for development objectives,

> Creating mutually beneficial techno-logistics infrastructure in a foreign land,

> Tackling the energy shortages arising due to poor energy infrastructure,

> Attaining self-sufficiency &employment generation at home,

> Demonstrating its robust and giant internationalistic posture of a Big brother in the region,

> Successfully positioning itself at a higher international diplomatic pedestal,

> Securing the support of big powers like USA and Russia and pose a deterrent to constantly increasing Chinese clout,

> Forming a multidimensional diplomatic alliance with Afghanistan, Iran and Japan to mark an effective Indian presence in the Chabahar SEZ and posing a potent deterrence to China-Pakistan combine.

Conclusion

It can, therefore, be safely understood, that energy security is an inseparable part of National Security and the diplomatic efforts of the Indian government of the day are proceeding aggressively in the right direction domestically as well as internationally in treating them as such. These positive& proactive efforts backed by a strong political stability of the government at home have a bright future especially considering the confidence and ease in handling international alliances which have come to be exhibited by the Indian leadership on every occasion.

Endnotes

1   Dwivedi Dhirendra, 'India's National Security Needs in the 21ˢᵗ Century' (ed) Prof ShekharAdhikai and Prof Sanjeev Bhadauria, Pentagon press (2014) (ISBN 978-81-8274-739-5)

2   Mahalingam, Sudha, *"India's Energy Security Challenges"* in "Strategising Energy: An Asian Perspective" (2014) (ed) SreematiGanguli(ISBN 978-93-81904-93-0)

3   https://sustainabledevelopment.un.org/content/documents/844 naturesjournal.pdf accessed on 29 April 2017)

4   *'India's National Security Needs in the 21ˢᵗ Century' (ed) Prof ShekharAdhikai and Prof Sanjeev Bhadauria, Pentagon press (2014) (ISBN 978-81-8274-739-5)*

5   Annual Report, Min of Petroleum & Natural Gas, Govt of India, 2015-16Page 42

6   Annual Report Min of Petroleum & Natural Gas 2016-17 Page 45

7   Sikri, Rajiv, Challenges and Strategy: Rethinking India's Foreign Policy, (2009), SAGE Publishing House, London (ISBN 978-81-321-1367-6

8   Linn, Johannes.F *"Central Asia Energy Challenges: Overcoming the Natural Resources Curse"* published in 2008

9   Roy, Meena Singh "North-South Corridor: Prospects and Challenges for India" compiled in the book titled *Central Asia and South Asia Energy Cooperation and Transport Linkages* published by Pentagon Press (ISBN 978-81-8374-551-1)

10 Dhall, Lt Col Vivek"India's Energy Security" (2013) Vij Books India Pvt Ltd, New Delhi

11 Pant, Girjesh"*India's emerging energy relations: Issues and Challenges*" Springer publications

12 Puntambekar, Ashish"*Indian Energy Security*" Indian Defence Review January-March 2008 issue

13 TOI New Delhi edition dated 24 May 16

14 Bakshi, Maj Gen (Dr) GD, "Chabahar Beltway will transform regional security architecture" published in Indian Military Review, Vol VII, 16 June 2016

15 Times of India, New Delhi dated 19 January 2017 (http://economictimes.indiatimes.com/news/politics-and-nation/five-things-about-chabahar-port-and-how-india-gains-from-it/articleshow/52400399.cms)

Local Democracy: Issues and Challenges of Economic Development in South Asia

Dr. Vadranam Suresh

Introduction

Many of the South Asian countries have empowered decentralised local government structures, recognising the need to localise and decentralise economic development. This enhanced focus on increasingly localised economic development is a global concern, which is currently gaining momentum[1]. As the Millennium Development Goals (MDGs) come to an end in 2015, the global debate on the post-2015 development agenda is already well underway. Unlike in the conception of the MDGs, local government, civil society, the private sector and other national, regional and international stakeholders have been far more engaged in the process than their successors. Following this extensive consultation, 17 Sustainable Development Goals (SDGs) have been drafted. With an increased focus on context specific and local economic development as a driver of poverty reduction, women's empowerment and 'inclusive growth with quality work' the world over, this is a great opportunity to ensure that local government and local economic development feature prominently in the strategy for implementing the new SDGs which promise to 'leave no one behind' and ensuring effective and accountable government 'at all levels'. This signals an important shift from a wholly top-down approach to a more bottom-up and localised approach which recognises the importance of local contexts and environments and of local governments as key actors in setting, monitoring and achieving the SDGs. There is also an emphasis on the ability of local governments to effectively implement and affect LED and positive local change, given the right policy framework, enabling environment and financial tools. With no common definition and limited sector-wide understanding of local economic development frameworks in South Asia, we need to instead look at a range of policies and activities that can reasonably be seen to make up local economic development in its different forms in South Asia. As such, it is necessary to look at what kind of LED activities and capacities are in place at the local level within local government; such as those that support agriculture and allied rural activities, small, micro and medium businesses and informal sector workers, such as urban street vendors[2].

Decentralization Processes

Political decentralization usually requires changes in constitutions and legal frameworks. Several South Asian countries in one way or another have moved ahead with political decentralization. Bangladesh, Bhutan, India, Maldives, Nepal, Pakistan, and Sri Lanka have adopted changes in their constitutions and legal framework to re-define the roles, functions and functionaries of local governments. There are different driving forces as to why these countries have pursued decentralization. The primary reason for this initiative, however, lies in the economic rationale that local governments, being closer to their constituencies, may be more responsive to local needs, and consequently, provide public services more efficiently[3].

Bangladesh has had a long history of rural local governments (the Union Parishads), although with limited powers and a long history of community-based systems of service delivery and Non-Governmental Organizations (NGOs). Bangladesh has been a parliamentary democracy since a constitutional amendment in 1991. The Constitution of Bangladesh, in Articles 59 and 60, has laid down a framework concerning local government bodies. After the elections in December 2008, the expectations have been that decentralization will be one of the pillars to enhance democracy and to reduce corruption[4]. In Bhutan, the Ninth Five-year Plan

(2002/03–2006/07) and tenth Five-year Plan (2008/09-2012/13) focused on the needs of the Gewogs (rural communities) and Dzongkhags (districts). Devolution of resources and decision-making powers to the local level is a key aim of the Plans. The 73rd and 74th Constitutional Amendments in India, issued in 1992, enshrined devolution in the Constitution of India and mandated that states hold regular elections and transfer funds and functions to the third tier of government— urban (i.e. municipalities) and rural (i.e. panchayats) local governments.[5] The constitutional sanction to local government has raised expectations and aspirations. Local Body elections have disproved the myth that women are uninterested in public life. There is a near unanimity among women that they would have been unable to get into these bodies were it not for statutory representation. Significantly, about 40 percent of women panchayat (rural local body) members belong to marginalized groups in the villages.[6]

Local government in Maldives provided for by the Decentralization Act 2010 and the Local Council Election Act 2010, and it is enshrined in the Constitution (Chapter VIII). The Local Government Authority Department of the Ministry of Home Affairs is responsible for local government, which comprises 20 atoll councils, 66 island councils and two city councils (Malé and Addu). Local government is in two tiers with the atoll councils in the first tier and the island and city councils in the second. Local elections are held every three years. The local authorities have revenue-raising powers, charging fees or rent for services provided, as well as receiving transfers from national government. They are also empowered to raise finance to fund development projects. Atoll councils are responsible for managing projects in the Atoll Development Plan not assigned to an island council. The island and city councils are responsible for primary health care, pre-school education, adult education, utilities, waste disposal, pest control and roads.[7]

In Nepal, the Local Self Government Act (LSGA) of 1999 defined three types of local bodies and endowed them with some revenue powers and expenditure responsibilities. Recently, Nepal has undergone a delicate transition from monarchy to the model of a federal state. In this context, the roles of the different tiers of government, the number of tiers, and the nature of fiscal flows are still under way to define the future of the decentralization strategy. Local bodies are becoming increasingly involved in local service provision and users' groups in the management of local resources and services. For example, thousands of user groups have been given authority to manage local forests. Decentralized governance has produced positive impacts in terms of people's participation in governance, poverty reduction, empowerment of women and weaker social groups, and involvement of non-governmental organizations and the private sector in the delivery of social and production services.[8]

Local government not only plays a role in implementing or directly supporting local economic development through projects but has at least as vital a role in creating an enabling environment for local business and the livelihoods of its citizens. For example, ensuring that basic infrastructure such as roads and electricity, health and education services are available to all, to ensure that it is relatively easy to start and 'do' business, and that complying with local regulations is straightforward and does not require bribes. Further, with a large part of the economic activity in South Asia being informal, it is of central concern that local government works with and enables informal economic factors, such as street vendors, in a proactive and inclusive manner. Local government can be seen therefore as far from being a passive regulator, more as an active stakeholder and driver of local economic development. Nevertheless, given the limited nature of local government in some of the countries, and the relative strength and importance of the third sector in providing access to basic services (especially in Bangladesh), The countries, whilst having a number of similarities within their local governance systems, are at different stages of development, with Maldives an upper middle-income country, Sri Lanka comfortably a middle income country, Pakistan and India lower middle income countries, and Bangladesh a low income country (World Bank 2014). Overall, the Commonwealth countries of South Asia are in a state of transition, change and uncertainty. Sri Lanka recently came out of a long civil war, and held presidential elections in 2010, strengthening the mandate of the then incumbent president Mahinda Rajapaksa who, after changing the constitution so he could run for a third term, narrowly lost in early 2015 to Maithripala Sirisena, one of his former ministers, running on an opposition coalition ticket .Pakistan is fighting an internal insurgency across large swathes of its territory, including the porous border areas near Afghanistan, resulting in security concerns across large parts of the country, and had its first democratic transition of power after elections held in May, 2013 when Nawaz Sharif took over as prime minister. Bangladesh meanwhile, suffered violent protests and a standstill, during and after highly contested elections in January, 2014 which returned the incumbent Sheikh Hasina amidst an election boycott from the opposition. India concluded largely peaceful elections with a change of government, and Narendra Modi becoming the new prime minister, in May, 2014[9]. While local economic development is prevalent in the region, the terminology LED is not widely used. Often local governments are not aware of their legal responsibilities for local economic development or those programmes in place at State/Provincial or National level to support local economic development initiatives. Local economic development is a process that brings together different partners in a local area to work together and harness local resources for sustainable economic growth. There is no single model for local economic development; approaches should reflect local needs and circumstances. LED creates an enabling environment for business and other stakeholders to work to promote equitable and balanced local economic growth. Pro-poor and inclusive LED enables local government to address poverty, unemployment and social deprivation, including through strategies for promoting youth employment, empowering disadvantaged and marginalised communities, support for skills development, and promotion of gender equity and equality (CLGF Cardiff Consensus) [10].

Overview of Local Economic Development in South Asia

Table 1. Nature of Local Government in South Asia

Country	Policy Framework	Local Government in Practice
Bangladesh	Local government is protected through Chapter three of the Constitution. The Zila Parishad Act 2000, the Local Government (Upazila Parishad) Act 1998, the Local Government (Union Parishad) Act 2000, the Local Government (Pourashava) Act 2009, the Local Government (City Corporation Act 2009 and the Hill District Council Act 1989 lay out responsibilities and powers. LG has four tiers: Zila Parishads, Upazila Parishads and Union Parishads.	The local government is active throughout Bangladesh, and it is overseen by the National government
India	The 73rd and 74th constitutional amendments in 1992 recognised local government, under Article 243 G of the Indian constitution, and the states are supposed to ensure delegation of responsibilities and Devolution of power to the local governments. Additionally, each state has its own legal framework to guide local governance	Local government is active across India. The 73rd & 74th constitutional amendments led to wider participation and citizen awareness at the local level, citizens' charters are also used to streamline participation. Additionally, organising community structures such as Rural and Urban

		National Livelihood Missions are operated at the local level.
Maldives	Local government is two-tier, comprising island councils and city councils, both are accountable to an A toll council. The Decentralisation Act passed in 2010 formalised the roles and responsibilities of Atoll and Island Councils and required that they be Democratically elected.	The legal framework for local governance is recently in place and local government is in place across the country.
Pakistan	18th Constitutional amendment, and provincial LG Acts from 2010 and 2013 require Local Government elections. The LG are not applicable in FATA.	In spite of planned elections, elections have been postponed in all provinces except Balochistan.
Sri Lanka	The 13th amendment to the constitution brought in the local government. Under the nine second-tier provincial council authorities governed by the Provincial Councils Act 1987, there are 23 municipal councils, 41 urban councils and 271 rural pradeshiya sabhas. The local authorities are governed by the Urban Councils Ordinance 1939, the Municipal Councils Ordinance 1947 and the Pradeshiya Sabhas Act (No.15) 1987.	The local authorities oversee duties related to the public health, utility services and roads. Pradeshiya sabhas have some additional developmental responsibilities. Moreover, the local authorities can also create by-laws albeit subject to approval by the minister of the provincial council.

Table 2. Fiscal Devolution across South Asia

Country	Policy	% LG in all govt. Expenditure 2014
Bangladesh	All fiscal decisions are controlled at the national level with very limited funds raised through local government levied taxes.	6.7%
India	The councils are empowered to levy house and land taxes and borrow a limited amount of money. Other sources of revenue include special projects and fundraising through events. There is a provision for the issue of tax-free municipal bonds to bring in investments from the private sector.	1.5% (Urban)
Maldives	Fiscal devolution is still being implemented. Substantial fiscal autonomy can be transferred to Councils, although central government can still control the Finances of the local councils.	Not available
Pakistan	Funds for LG are derived from provincial government, which in turn relies on national government for more than 80% of funds.	Not available
Sri Lanka	Local authorities are responsible for the collection of levies and taxes, property rates and assessment taxes as well as rents. However, none of the tax rates that the local governments levy are set by them.	Not available

Table 3. Nature of Local Economic Development across South Asia

Country	Understanding of LED	Drivers of LED
Bangladesh	Government of Bangladesh recognises the importance of driving economic development through local governing bodies as evident from its efforts to strengthen the Local Government. Division (LGD) to implement social, economic and infrastructure development activities.	NGOs are driving local development in Bangladesh. The priorities set for LED are made by the national government. Most projects and policies related to economic development are related to agriculture, forests and fisheries, trade and industry as well as Tourism.
India	The Strategy undertaken for Economic development in India by different stakeholders is different, especially between the rural and urban areas. However, there is an emphasis on the need for economic development at the local level across the country, in both rural and urban areas. Many economic development projects rely on the involvement of local government (e.g. the National Rural Livelihoods Mission)	Most initiatives by local government in rural areas focus on improving farming practices, developing market access by value chain development and encouraging rural enterprises, including setting up cooperatives. There is also an emphasis on MSMEs development through the cluster development approach to build market linkages and improve production efficiency. In addition, microfinance-led microenterprises development is common, following the success of the SHG-Bank Linkage Programme for the Poor by NABARD. In the urban there is growing focus on Skill development through PPPs with industry.

Maldives	The Strategic Action Plan (SAP) 7 dated 2009 governs all development in the Maldives. The key themes of the SAP include good governance, social justice and economic development with all the strategies verified for climate change resilience. The decentralisation of public health was the first service to be transferred to the local bodies, in 2011.	The Government aims to achieve decentralisation in two phases. The first focuses on establishing provincial offices, local councils, initiating programmes to address immediate capacity building and advocacy, and development of operational frameworks for coastal zone management and climate change adaptation.
Pakistan	Pakistan federal structure devolves issues of local and provincial development to the Provincial Government. The legislation is in transition in the four provincial local government acts.	The provinces can now drive local economic development. Local government has considerable mandate over local economic development, including health, education and infrastructure.
Sri Lanka	The government's National Development Policy Framework Vision, Mahinda Chintana 2011-2016, lays out the importance of inclusive and local development while developing core economic sectors (agriculture, fisheries, livestock, irrigation, plantations, and tourism), enterprises, physical infrastructure as well as human capital. There is	The District and Divisional Secretariat Offices (DSOs) seem to be at the centre of all successful initiatives implemented by the local governments, especially those relating to economic development, reflecting strong integration within the different tiers of the government.

	limited clarity on how the local level governments and authorities will be involved in this process.	The third sector is active in fostering partnership between the local government and the community to drive inclusive local economic development. Many of the projects are focused in underserved regions.

Table 4. Examples of Local Economic Development across South Asia

Country	Type	Stakeholders and Action
Bangladesh	Private sector-NGOs	Ejab Group and Shiblee Hatchery & Farms are two examples of private enterprises that have taken up local economic development through improving the lives of the community they work with as a part of their business function.
India	Local government and NGO together with local entrepreneurs and small businesses.	The local governments in the state of Kerala partnered with the Local Economic Development Society (LEDS) based in Kochi to work with small producers and entrepreneurs and build successful enterprises and collectives.
Maldives	Government is looking to develop local government projects.	There are proposed projects, for instance for energy but this is not yet in action.

Pakistan	Donor-funded poverty alleviation fund.	The Livelihood, Enterprise and Employment Development (LEED) under Pakistan Poverty Alleviation Fund (PPAF) works to support entrepreneurship development on a large scale.
Sri Lanka	Donors	The Northern Livelihood Development Project (N-LDP), a part of an EU-led programme, works with the conflict-affected communities, particularly those socially and economically excluded, in the Jaffna, Killinochchi and Mullaithivu districts

Local Economic Development in India

India's last general elections, held in 2014, saw the highest ever voter turnout with a change in power, with aspirations of economic growth and development. With a high level of inequality, there is a wide need for stakeholders to contribute to reducing the gap. The country already has a vibrant civil society and a history of rural local governing bodies known as Panchayats along with a vibrant cooperative movement, which has resulted in improvement in rural income.[11] There is also an increasing urbanisation and while the local governance system was originally designed for a country with a clear urban and rural divide, these recent transitions call for structures that are evolving to adapt to these chan. While the 73rd and 74th constitutional amendment Acts in 1992 recognised and empowered local government, under Article 243 G of the Indian constitution the states are tasked with ensuring delegation of responsibilities and devolution of power to the local governments. Additionally, each state has its own legal framework to guide local governance.[12] Election processes are usually guided by the law defined by the states in keeping with the inclusive and consultative structures within the governance hierarchy to ensure monitoring the delivery of services.[13] In both urban and rural areas, all councillors are directly elected by a first-past-the-post system for a five-year tenure with a minimum one-third of all seats reserved for women (many states have reserved 50%) as well as reservation for scheduled castes and scheduled tribes.[14] Mayors get elected directly or indirectly for either one or five years, depending on the state. The position of mayor/chairperson is also assigned to vulnerable groups on a rotating basis. All municipalities with a population over 300,000 needs to establish ward committees chaired by the local ward councillor. Of the 2.9 million elected representatives to the three levels of panchayats, about 42.3 percent are women, 13.70 percent belong to SCs and 14.6 percent are STs in 2013.[15] Uttar Pradesh state had the highest number of elected women representatives while their number was lowest in Goa. While the *Zila Parishads* have elected councillors, president and vice-president, its administrative machinery is headed by a Chief Executive Officer or District Magistrate who is either an Indian Administrative Service Officer or a State Civil Service Officer. While the 73[rd]and 74th amendments to the constitution have led to wider participation and citizen awareness at the local level, citizens' charters are also used to streamline participation[16] there are also schemes for organising community structures such as National Rural Livelihood Mission and National Urban Livelihood Mission. Moreover, many states expect the cities to create area *sabhas* at the grassroots level to promote bottom-up planning and management of assets. There are associations in place to ensure interactions between local government bodies at national, state and local level. Some of the state level associations for local governments include Kerala Grama Panchayath Association, Orissa State Panchayat Association, and Jharkhand State Panchayat Association. There are also women leader's state-level associations in some states like Goa Panchayat Mahila Shakti Abhiyan (GPMSA) and Panchayat Mahila Shakti Abhiyan of Maharashtra State. Apart from state-level organisations of elected representatives, or city managers' associations, national level associations include the All India Council of Mayors (the municipal corporations) as well as *Nagar Palik Pramukh Sangthen* (other urban municipalities).[17] Further, the Gram Sabha (made up of registered voters form the village) is mandated to undertake governance of panchayats, as noted in the Panchayat Extension to Schedule Area Act 1996. The Gram Sabha is where plans for the work of the Gram Panchayat are placed before the local community. The Gram Sabha acts as checks and balances, and ensures transparency in the work carried out by the panchayats. In other words, it keeps an eye on elected representatives. In 2004, a separate Ministry of Panchayati Raj was created to oversee the implementation of constitutional policies related to *Panchayati Raj*. While most of the duties and responsibilities, including framing policies related to local governance rest with the state governments, the Ministry aims to support the Panchayats through advocacy and funding as well as technical and capacity building assistance. Additionally, the Ministries for urban development, housing and urban poverty alleviation, and rural development are guided by constitutional provisions and are responsible for developing a nationwide policy for their sector which the local government bodies are expected to adhere to. The ministries also participate in preparing model Acts, laws, by-laws, manuals, guidelines, checklists and capacity-building programmes for various functions. At the state level, there is a minister responsible for local government to supervise the administration of the relevant legislation propagated at the state level. In extraordinary circumstances, the minister or state government have the power to dissolve local government bodies, and govern them directly for up to six months, though this provision is rarely used.[18]

The government of India clearly demarcates between rural and urban areas, and as discussed earlier, they are governed by different legal frameworks as well, drawing from the 73rd and 74th amendments. The local government system is therefore split between urban (Municipalities) and rural councils (panchayats). However, there are overlaps in terms of development needs, and many rural areas are transitioning to semi-urban areas with changing needs. The 74th Constitutional Amendment Act provides for three types of municipalities depending on the size and area, namely: *Nagar panchayats* for areas in transition from rural to urban, municipal councils for smaller urban areas, and municipal corporations for larger urban areas. In the urban areas, the municipal corporations have a range of committees based on their core functions which take account of finance, education, water supply and sanitation. While these committees are for the purpose of deliberations and consultations, the decision making power rests with the councils who have the option to establish a wide range of other committees. In each state the authorities of the mayors and executive committees differ because they are determined by the respective state municipal acts.[19]

As seen in the figure, the panchayats are the local governing bodies with either two, three or single tier structure depending on their population. There is a division of duties between the tiers including a limited coordination role for higher levels of the *panchayati* authorities. The most State law sets up mandatory committees, however, these are different across the different states. The *Zilla Parishads* are also required establishing committees for finance and audit, planning, social justice, education, health, agriculture and industries. Additionally, the gram panchayats have production, social justice and amenities committees.

Urban Councils

While funds from the state governments partially support the infrastructure projects carried out by municipal governments, there is a provision for the issue of tax-free municipal bonds to bring in investments from the private sector including financial institutions, with the Pooled Finance Development Fund providing credit enhancement grants. The size of municipal expenditure as part of GDP has declined from 1.7% in 1998/99 to 1.5% in 2007/08, making the share of the municipal budget in the total budget of centre, states and urban local governments around 4%.Additionally, municipal councils are empowered to levy house and land taxes and borrow a limited amount of money. Other sources of revenue include special projects and fund raising through events. Cities contribute nearly two-thirds of the total national tax revenue due to the large proportion of taxes, fees, etc., collected from urban centres. Further, the 13th Finance Commission recommends that the maximum limit of profession tax collectible should be raised from the present value of INR 2,500 per annum and permit the local bodies to levy tax on the properties of the Central Government[20].

Rural Councils

The state governments are required by law to review the financial position of the panchayats and urban local governments every five years in consultation with their state finance commission and make recommendations for the subsequent term. The 11th Central Finance Commission (2000-05) started to make recommendations relating to local bodies and referred to the measures needed to augment the consolidated funds of states to supplement the resources of panchayats and municipalities on the basis of the recommendations made by the Finance Commissions of the concerned states. Moreover, to proportionately share the divisible pool of the central revenue, the 13th Central Finance Commission (2010-15) increased the volume of transfers to local government to INR 23,111 bn, a 400% increase, by recommending a General Basic Grant (GBG). The GBG was to be made from the divisible pool of national government funds amounting to 1.5%, and performance grants amounting to 0.5% for 2011/12, and 1% of the divisible pool thereafter. The disbursement to the states and to the local bodies thereafter was phased. For rural areas, 4% of the divisible pool is proposed to be allotted to local bodies and earmarked for a range of activities.[21]

Local Economic Development

The strategy undertaken for economic development in India by different stakeholders varies, especially between the rural and urban areas. Most initiatives by the local government in rural areas are focused on improving farming practices, developing market access for farmers by value chain development and encouraging rural enterprises. This includes setting up cooperatives for rural producers to build their bargaining power and undertake collective economic development. There has also been an emphasis on the MSMEs development through the Cluster development approach in order to build market linkages and improve production efficiency. Additionally, the microfinance-led microenterprises development has also been used extensively especially after the success of SHG-Bank Linkage Programme for the Poor by the National Bank for Agriculture and Rural Development (NABARD). More recently, in the urban areas, there is a growing focus on skills development and making it relevant to local industry through public-private partnerships.[22] The National Skill Development Council, for instance, is a public-private partnership initiative by the Government of India to build skills in core sectors like agriculture, automobile manufacture, healthcare, civil engineering, construction and real estate, among others. It partners with training service providers and companies for capacity building and placements. It also factors in the needs of the urban local bodies and works with them to support through meeting their skills related needs, such as resource requirements for various projects under the Jawaharlal Nehru National Urban Renewal Mission (JnNURM) including infrastructure, basic services to urban poor (BSUP) and Capacity Building and Institutional Development (CBID). While both urban and rural local bodies are conferred with responsibilities towards local economic development, there is a clear distinction between the type of activities they take up and the support they need. For example, one of the primary economic development activities that the Panchayat support is agriculture through linkages to district level markets for village level cooperatives. The cities, on the other hand, seem to focus. The strategy undertaken for economic development in India by different stakeholders varies, especially between the rural and urban areas. Most initiatives by the local government in rural areas are focused on improving farming practices, developing market access for farmers by value chain development and encouraging rural enterprises. This includes setting up cooperatives for rural producers to build their bargaining power and undertake collective economic development. There has also been an emphasis on the MSMEs development through the Cluster development approach in order to build market linkages and improve production efficiency. Additionally, the microfinance-led microenterprises development has also been used extensively especially after the success of SHG-Bank Linkage Programme for the Poor by the National Bank for Agriculture and Rural Development (NABARD). More recently, in the urban areas, there is a growing focus on skills development and making it relevant to local industry through public-private partnerships.[23]

Nature of LED in India

On transportation as a primary driver to support economic development Article 243 G of the Indian constitution protects the provision for the devolution of power to the local bodies by the State Legislative Assemblies and this includes functions related to economic development. The policy provides for the devolution of powers and responsibilities to Panchayats at the appropriate level relating to designing and implementing plans for economic development and social justice as well as the implementation of Centrally-funded schemes for economic development and social justice. Further, in terms of responsibilities related to enabling local economic development, at the Union level the Ministry for Urban Development, Housing and Urban Poverty Alleviation and the Ministry for Panchayati Raj and Rural Development oversee the respective functions of local government.[24]

Gram Panchayat's e-panchayat Initiative

The government of India has initiated a programme to digitise local panchayats across the country, through the Digital Panchayat e-platform and with the support of the Digital Empowerment Foundation (DEF) together with the National Internet Exchange of India (NIXI), Government of India. The goal is for each panchayat to have a website that improves the functioning of the panchayats and their service delivery, as well as to provide information about the Panchayat and services. The aim is also to strengthen and empower local communities as regards local government governance and transparency. Chandama Gram Panchayat has a website which provides recent news, purview of services, including a database of all residents. Punsari Gram Panchayat, meanwhile, showcases the local village, and provides information about all the members of the gram panchayat, among other things. Lastly, the Hiware Bazar e-panchayat website provides background and history of the village, information about the panchayat, and details of its many different development schemes and their effectiveness, something that the village panchayat is proud given its official status as a model village. An important side effect of the e-panchayat initiative is that it raises awareness of the internet among panchayat members, in turn enabling access to information that members may not have been able to access previously. What each of these pioneering village panchayats have in common, are leaders that are educated and relatively young. They have returned to their village'sand are keen to digitise in order to improve both local services, but also their villages' access to markets, or, for example, to attract tourism.[25]

Cooperatives

The National Policy on Cooperative (2002) emphasises the role that cooperatives can play in local economic development. There are cooperatives for agriculture credit, farm inputs, agriculture produce (sugar, wheat, milk, and oil), warehouse, fisheries, rubber and spices. The cooperatives have been successful in driving economic development at the grassroots level. India's 100,000 dairy cooperatives, for instance, collect 16.5 million litres of milk from 12 million farmer members every day, making a significant contribution to India's food supply. However, farmer cooperatives have yet to reach their full potential as they address their requirements for financing and technical support.[26]

National Agricultural Innovation Project aims to enable accelerated and sustainable transformation of Indian agriculture by public organizations in partnership with farmers, the private sector and other stakeholders so that it can support poverty alleviation and income generation through collaborative development and application of agricultural innovations. The Project focuses on the management of change in the agricultural research system, research on production to consumption systems, research on sustainable rural livelihood security, and basic and strategic research in frontier areas of agricultural sciences.

Rural Tourism

Various stakeholders, including enterprises are exploring the role of tourism in benefitting local communities and there is a role for the local governments to enable tourism-led economic development. There are prospects to improve the impact of tourism on local communities through training and employment generation. In fact, the Ministry of Tourism has introduced a scheme for rural tourism which plans to promote village tourism as the primary tourism product. The implementation is planned to be done through a Convergence Committee headed by the District Collector to carry out assisted activities like improving the environment, hygiene and infrastructure.[27]

Capacity Building for Local Entrepreneurship Development

Despite a strong framework for local economic development in Kerala, its projects relating to entrepreneurship development have not produced the desired results due to insufficient access to end-to-end support. To improve the success rate of enterprises and enhance their earning capacities, local governments in the state partnered with the Local Economic Development Society (LEDS) based in Kochi (Cochin) to work with small producers and entrepreneurs and build successful enterprises and collectives. LEDS has a team of professional managers from diverse organisational functions as well as sectors such as government, NGO, Cooperative and Corporate.[28]

Conclusion

It needs to be underlined that local government is not only practical but also effective in taking development directly to the people in this region. Therefore, it is imperative to make local government sustainable and help to reduce poverty and provide a variety of vital public services. Hence, a certain level of state intervention is necessary in order to ensure equitable distribution of the benefits, and social inclusivity. Further, local governments elected and monitored by the electorate who understand their rights or is sensitized enough to do so, local governments can be good medicine against bad governance, corruption, and ensuring efficient service delivery. In other words, local government is not just important for the delivery of services, but is crucial for the economic and social development of the people of South Asia, especially in the context of its present socio-economic situation. Therefore, for development to be successful at local level it needs to be backed by political will, clear legal responsibilities for local government, appropriate instruments, and ensuring that it is grounded in local conditions

It is clear that India is the country in South Asia with the most examples of local government led local economic development initiatives and projects. In addition, local economic development is enabled through country-wide initiatives such as e-panchayats as well as through national programmes that are delivered through local government. These include delivering national schemes for economic growth and poverty reduction, and some council are already planning and delivering local economic development programmes such as market development, business stakeholder forums and support for local cooperative development. At the same time, it is important for local government to engage the private sector, for instance through public-private partnerships (PPP). There are local governments leveraging their unique position to get the private sector to provide services, such as cleaning, road sweeping and rubbish collection. Local government needs to increase its focus on creating enabling environments for entrepreneurship and business locally. This is especially timely given that governments across the region are currently emphasising the need for more entrepreneurial economies, where innovation and new and growing business plays a major role. Levels of bureaucracy are a barrier to LED, and the mindset of local bureaucrats at times stifle the 'ease of doing business' locally, such as excessive 'red tape', complexity and time taken to start and register a business, difficulty in obtaining permits, subsidies, information about rules and regulations and so forth. More broadly, local government can do much to attract and enable business by working to ensure infrastructure such as electricity and internet, as well as adequate water and sanitation facilities, and develop markets or market access. Some examples, such as markets in Karachi, and the e-panchayat initiative in India, show that local Government can be successful in creating enabling business environments.

However, national (and provincial/state) governments have important responsibilities and roles in enabling the policy and regulatory framework for creating enabling business environments at the local level. For instance, national government should support local government efforts to create an enabling environment through infrastructure, connectivity, roads and electricity programmes. National initiatives such as tax holidays, special economic zones and special dispensations for backwards areas, for instance, can help. Its needful to additional initiatives that can be helpful include investment promotion and decentralising foreign investment. Likewise, labour market policies may need to be adapted at the state/provincial or national level to better fit with current business needs.

Endnotes

1 Ahmad, M. S., & Talib, N. B "Local Government Systems and Decentralization: Evidence from Pakistan's Devolution Plan", Faculty of Management & Finance, University of Finance &Manage ment,Warsaw&VizjaPress&IT,2013

2 Slack, L. "The Post-2015 Global Agenda –A Role for Local Govt". *Commonwealth Journal of Local Governance*2014

3 Cheema,A.,Khan,A.Q.,Myerson,R.B. "Breaking the Countercyclical Pattern of Local Democracy in Pakistan", University of Chicago, 2014

4 CLGF "The Local Government System in Bangladesh" *Country profile*www.clgf.org.uk/Bangladesh, 2013

5 CLGF "The Local Government System in Pakistan". *Country Profile.* www.clgf.org.uk/pakistan, 2013

6 Paul, S., & Goel, P. R. "Decentralisation in Bangladesh", NCAR2010, September

7   CLGF "The Local Government System in Maldives" *Country Profile*www.clgf.org.uk/Maldives, 2013

8   Denis,E.,Mukhopadhyay,P.,&Zérah,M..H. "Subaltern Urbanisation in India",*Economic & Political Weekly*, 2012, 52-62.

9   Reddy, P., & Wallis,M.."Energising Local Economies: Local Economic Development around the Commonwealth". *Background discussion paper for the 2011 Commonwealth Local Government Conference* Cardiff: CLGF.2011

10 CLGF,"The Local Government System in India",*Country Profile*. www.clgf.org.uk/india: CLGF, 2013

11 Alok, V. N. "Role of Panchayat Bodies in Rural Development Since 1959". *Theme Paper for the Fifty-Fifth Members' Annual Conference.* Indian Institute of Public Administration, 2011

12 Alam, M., & Wajidi, A. M. "Pakistan's Devolution of Power Plan 2001: A Brief Dawn for Local Democracy?"*Commonwealth Journal of Local Governance, 2013,*Issue 12, May, 20-34.

13 Deshpande, C., Mizunoya, & Miyuki7 CLGF,"The Local Government System in Maldives"*Country Profile*www.clgf.org.uk/Maldives, 2013

14 Lall, S. V., Chakravorty, & Sanjoy. "Industrial Location and Spatial Inequality: Theory and Evidence from India",*Review of Development Economics 2005, 9 (1)*, 47–68.

15 Heideman, L,"From Words to Action. SALARInternational Section SALGAEconomic Development and Planning", ALAN and BALA, 2012, February

16 Hassan, M., & Prichard, W. "The Political Economy of Tax Reform in Bangladesh: Political Settlements, Informal Institutions and the Negotiation of Reform",*ICTD Working Paper 14.* IDS,2013, November

17 Lall, S. V., Wang, H. G., & Deichmann, U,"Infrastructure and City Competitiveness in India", *Working Paper*2010/22, UNU-WIDER

18 Novosad, P., & Asher, S. "Politics and Local Economic Growth: Evidence from India", Harvard University, 2013

19 Treller, G. E. "Building Community Prosperity Through Local

Economic Development: An Introduction to LED Principles and Practices", Ukraine Municipal Local Economic Development, 2013

20 Smoke, P., Loffler, G.,& Bosi,G. "The Roleof Decentralisation/ Devolution in Improving Development Outcomes at the Local Level: Review of the Literature and Selected Cases" DFID& Local Development International LLC, 2013

21 United Cities and Local Governments 2013,"Basic Services for all in an Urbanizing World", GOLD II UCLG, 2013

22 Alok, V. N. 'Strengthening of Panchayats in India: Comparing Devolution across States -Empirical Assessment -2012-13". The Indian Institute of Public Administration and Ministry of Panchayati Raj, Government of India, 2013

23 Shafqat, S. "Local Government Acts 2013 and Province-Local Government Relations" United Nations Development Programme. *UNDP Commentary:* Accessed on September 12, 2014

24 Budds, J. "The Role of Local Government in LED: A Step-by-step Approach" Developed by VNG International. The Hague, The Netherlands, 2007

25 Empel, C. V. "Local Economic Development in Polonnaruwa District, Sri Lanka",*The Good Practice LED Cases in South Asia Under the ROAP LED Product Line of 2007.* ILO, 2008, April

26 Helmsing, A. H. "Local Economic Development: New Generations of Actors, Policies and Instruments",*A Summary Report Prepared for the UNCDF Symposium on Decentralization Local Governance in Africa.* ISS, The Hague, 2001

27 Wekwete, K. "Local Government and Local Economic Development in Southern Africa", CLGF, 2014

28 UNICEF, "Study on the Decentralisation Process in the Maldives" UNICEF, Maldives, 2013

Contributors

Dr. Jyotika Teckchandani is currently an Assistant Professor at the Amity Institute of Social Sciences, Amity University, Uttar Pradesh. She did her Bachelors and Masters in Political Science from Sri Venkateswara College and from Lady Shri Ram College. She received her M.Phil. and Ph.D. degrees from the Centre of West Asian Studies, JMI, New Delhi.

She is the author of the books Islam and Gender Politics in Iran, State and Women in Islamic Republic of Iran: Khomeini Era (1979–89), Handbook of Political Science and International relations, Politics and Development in India: Internal and External Dimensions and recently released India in World Affairs: Emerging Trends.

Besides, she has contributed a number of articles in academic journals of repute and newspapers including Indian Journal of Secularism, Journal of West Asian Studies, Quest International Multidisciplinary Research Journal, International Education and Research Journal, Journal of Social Science and Humanities Research, International Journal of Advanced Research, Social Sciences International Research Journal, The Pioneer, The Quint, Hardnews, India Samvaad, Wion, Rajasthan Patrika, Millenium Post etc.Her research interests include Gender Politics, Foreign Policy analysis, Indian and West Asian Politics.

VC Shushant Parashar is a Ph.D. Research Scholar in Political Science, at the Amity Institute of Social Sciences, Amity University. His thesis focuses on Environmental Security Policy in context to the South Asian region with emphasis on India and Bhutan. He has written and presented papers on the same topic at many conferences. His research interests include politics and environment with reference to South Asia. He has completed his MPhil in South and Southeast Asian Studies from University of Madras, Chennai. He has completed his M.A. in South Asian Studies from UMISARC, Pondicherry University, Pondicherry. He has done his graduation in Bachelors of Journalism and Mass Communication, ASCO, Amity University.

Dr. Nandini Sahay is working as Assistant Professor Social Work, at Amity University. She has been involved in the education sector, counselling and social work for about a decade now. Her passion for social work connects her to her immediate surrounding and community. She holds a doctorate degree in Social Work. She is a good orator and keen thinker. She writes regularly on different dimensions of women empowerment especially on reproductive rights of women. Her articles and research papers are published in international and national journals which include Yojna, Kuruchhetra, TeraGreen and in national newspapers. In recent past, she has been invited by a series of channels like ABP News, NDTV and Zee News to speak on social issues.

Dr. Suresh Chandra Patel, M.A.,M.Phil., PhD, is presently working as an Assistant Professor of Political Science in the Post Graduate Department of Political Science and Public Administration, Sambalpur University, Jyoti Vihar, Burla, Odisha. He is a life member of Indian Political Science Association and Odisha Political Science Association .He is teaching Political Science for the last 27 years. He has participated and presented papers in more than 80 National and International Conferences. More ever, he has chaired a number of National and International Conferences. He has also received the Best speaker award in a Conference Organized by ISDR, Ranchi, Jharkhand and is known as a good Orator.

Deblina Mukherjee is an Assistant Professor in Political Science attached to West Bengal Education Service, Government of West Bengal, India since July 2014 and is currently posted at Jhargram Raj College, Girls' Wing, West Bengal. She acquired her Bachelor of Arts degree in Political Science in 2011, Master of Arts degree in Political Science with International Relations in 2013 and M.

Phil in International Relations in 2015 from Jadavpur University, Kolkata, West Bengal, India. She has also been engaged in academic counselling in Political Science and Public Administration and is attached to Netaji Subhas Open University, West Bengal, India as a Counsellor from July, 2015 onwards.

Puspitarani Bardhan is a MANF Research Scholar, M.A, M.PHIL, Ph.D. (Continuing) in P.G. Deptt of Political Science and Public Administration, Sambalpur University, JyotiVihar, Burla, Odisha. I am a keen researcher and doing my Ph.D. work. I have some publication as article and am presented papers in different international and national seminars and conferences. My area of research is in Maoist in India, but I have interested in good governance, terrorism and international relation also. I have teaching experience of 4 years and has been vowed to writing and research since very beginning.

Rajneesh Kumar earned his Master's degree in Political Science & International Relations in First division with a "Certificate of Merit" from University of Allahabad in 1988. A Fellow of the University Grants Commission, he also obtained his second Master's degree in Journalism & Mass Communication with 'A' Grading in January 2016 from Sikkim Manipal University. An avid reader with an innate flair for writing, he has a few academic papers to his credit apart from having written for print media from 1986-1991. He is presently serving as Director in the Government of India and has special interest in contemporary issues related to National Security, Military & Media relations, Nation building and Globalization. He is also concurrently pursuing Doctoral studies in Political Science from Amity University (Uttar Pradesh).

Dr. Vadranam Suresh presently working as Post-Doctoral Fellow, (Indian Council of Social Science Research (ICSSR), New Delhi, Ministry of Human Resource Development, Government of India) Department of Politics and International Studies, Pondicherry Central University, Puducherry. Former Assistant Professor and Head Department of Public Administration, Valluvar College of Science and Management, Karur. He is an expert in Local Governments, Public Policy, Development Administration and

International Relations. He visited South Asian Countries. He got 10 years of teaching and research experience. He obtained his M.A. Degree in Public Administration from Acharya Nagarjuna University, Andhra Pradesh, M.Phil. and Ph.D. in Political Science and Public Administration from Annamalai University, Tamilnadu. He has published number of books and articles in national and international reputed journals.

Index

www.ingramcontent.com/pod-product-compliance
Lightning Source LLC
Chambersburg PA
CBHW031543260326
41914CB00002B/252